A Guide to Ethics and Public Policy

Developed by D. Don Welch during his 28 years of teaching ethics and public policy, the rationale behind *A Guide to Ethics and Public Policy* is to present a comprehensive guide for making policy judgments.

Rather than present specific cases that raise moral issues or discuss the role a few concepts play in the moral analysis of policy, this book instead provides a broad framework for the moral evaluation of public policies and policy proposals. This framework is organized around five guiding principles: benefit, effectiveness, fairness, fidelity, and legitimacy. These principles identify the factors that should be taken into account and the issues that should be addressed as citizens deal with the question of what the United States government, or any other governing body, should do. Organized by concept, with illustrations and examples frequently interspersed, the book covers both theory and specific issues.

A Guide to Ethics and Public Policy outlines a comprehensive ethical framework, provides content to the meaning of the five principles that comprise that framework through the use of illustrations and examples, and offers guidance about how to navigate one's way through the conflicts and dilemmas that inevitably result from a serious effort to analyze policies.

D. Don Welch was Associate Dean and Professor of Law and Religion at Vanderbilt University from 1984 to 2012. His book grows out of a career divided between law and ethics, especially in the experiences of 28 years of teaching law students, followed by service on the staff of St. Augustine's Chapel at Vanderbilt.

D1564738

A Guide to Ethics and Public Policy
Finding Our Way

D. Don Welch

Routledge
Taylor & Francis Group

NEW YORK AND LONDON

First published 2014
by Routledge
711 Third Avenue, New York, NY 10017

and by Routledge
2 Park Square, Milton Park, Abingdon, Oxon OX14 4RN

Routledge is an imprint of the Taylor & Francis Group, an informa business

Library of Congress Cataloging in Publication Data
Welch, Don, 1947–
  A guide to ethics and public policy : finding our way / D. Don
  Welch.
    pages cm
  1. Public administration—United States—Moral and ethical
  aspects.   2. United States—Politics and government—Moral
  and ethical aspects.   3. Political ethics—United States.   I. Title.
  JF1525.E8W43 2014
  172—dc23   2013040786

ISBN: 978–1–138–01377–3 (hbk)
ISBN: 978–1–138–01379–7 (pbk)
ISBN: 978–1–315–79509–6 (ebk)

Typeset in Bembo
by RefineCatch Limited, Bungay, Suffolk, UK

Printed and bound in the United States of America by Publishers Graphics, LLC on sustainably sourced paper.

To Les and Jordan
who make me think

Contents

Acknowledgements   ix

1 Introduction   1

2 Ethical Discourse and Public Policy   7
Talking about Ethics 8
Achieving Results 10
Obeying Rules 12
Responding to Others 14
Five Benchmarks 17
Appeals to Emotion 24
A Preview 28

3 Defining the Good: Benefit   32
What Is a Benefit? 32
Which Benefits? Pragmatic Concerns 35
Which Benefits? Principled Concerns 38
Public Preferences: Preference-Based Utilitarianism 44
Experts: Welfare-Based Utilitarianism 50
A Dynamic Interaction 53
Benefit-Based Policymaking 55

4 Stewardship of Resources: Effectiveness   58
Tradeoffs among Outcomes 58
Effective Means 61
Effectiveness and Popular Control 63
Limitations on the Reach of Effectiveness 68
Making Policy with Imperfect Information 72
Behavioral Economics: The Endowment Effect 75

5 Serving Justice: Fairness   79

Multiple Criteria 80
Types of Fairness Standards 83
The Liberty Baseline 86
The Welfare Baseline 88
Choosing a Baseline? 90
Fairness in Different Contexts 92

6 Honoring Commitments: Fidelity   97

Commitments Made 99
Structural Requirements 100
Presumed Obligations 103
External Assumptions 105
The Ideal of Public Service 109

7 Ownership of Problems: Legitimacy   112

Moral Assessments of Legitimacy 114
Sorting Through the Options 124

8 Benchmarks and Moral Discernment   129

Conflicting Norms 129
What's Going On? 130
Understanding Benchmarks 132
Moral Discernment 134
Embracing Humility 135
Passion and Compassion 137
Living in Community 139

Benediction   144

Sources Cited   146
Index   150

Acknowledgements

I must acknowledge the teachers who introduced me to the study of ethics: Dan McGee, James Sellers and Howard Harrod. I chose my career path in the hope that I could, in some small measure, do for others what these teachers did for me. I also acknowledge a debt to Amy Gutmann and Dennis Thompson, neither of whom I have ever met. Teaching out of their *Ethics and Politics* book through four editions was a continually enlightening experience, and inspired me to try to find all the pieces of the puzzle.

I value the contributions of the students I taught for 28 years at Vanderbilt Law School. Many of them were subjected to early drafts of the manuscript that eventually became this book. I suspect that I learned more from them than they learned from me. The friends and colleagues who read early versions, offered advice, and pointed me in constructive directions include Taylor Wray, Doug Knight, Jim Doramus and James Gooch.

My colleagues at Routledge Press—Michael Kerns, Darcy Bullock, John Clarke, Eileen Power and Heather Cushing—were unfailing in their professionalism and paved the way to this finished product.

My greatest thanks goes to Celeste. Without her unswerving support and encouragement this book would never have seen the light of day.

We hold these truths to be self-evident, that all men are created equal, that they are endowed by their Creator with certain unalienable rights, that among these are Life, Liberty, and the pursuit of Happiness. That to secure these rights, Governments are instituted among Men, deriving their just powers from the consent of the governed.

—United States Declaration of Independence

We the People of the United States, in Order to form a more perfect Union, establish Justice, insure domestic Tranquility, provide for the common defence, promote the general Welfare, and secure the Blessings of Liberty to ourselves and our Posterity, do ordain and establish this Constitution for the United States of America.

—Constitution of the United States of America

It is for us the living, rather, to be dedicated here to the unfinished work which they who fought here have thus far so nobly advanced. It is rather for us to be here dedicated to the great task remaining before us—that from these honored dead we take increased devotion to that cause for which they gave the last full measure of devotion—that we here highly resolve that these dead shall not have died in vain—that this nation, under God, shall have a new birth of freedom—and that government of the people, by the people, for the people, shall not perish from the earth.

—Abraham Lincoln, Gettysburg Address

1   Introduction

If you think that all of the good arguments in any public policy debate are on your side, you probably haven't thought enough. This book presents a framework for thinking about public policy—thinking deeply and broadly and carefully. What should the government do about terrorism, health care, education, unemployment, deficit spending, energy independence, climate change, and a host of other issues? Serious efforts to figure out answers to such questions encounter mountains of data, unknowable futures, with one complexity piled on top of another. When we look for guidance, the path is often cluttered with dueling experts and bombastic media stars who are more interested in generating heat than in shedding light.

In such a world, it is not surprising when citizens retreat to simplifying slogans and knee-jerk ideologies. The purpose of this book is to provide an alternative, to offer a framework for answering questions about what our government ought to do. The conclusions we reach about what our government should do are fundamentally moral choices. Many of our public policy debates are so contentious, and seemingly without end, because important and conflicting moral values can be found on all sides of virtually any public policy discussion. This reality should not induce paralysis, but should prod us to extend ourselves, to reach beyond readily apparent or comfortable solutions.

In the public policy world, we do not have the option of refusing to make a decision. When we choose not to decide we are, in reality, making a choice in favor of the status quo. Sometimes choosing the status quo is appropriate. After all, the present situation is the result of prior choices, and surely many of those prior choices were good ones. But when the status quo is affirmed, that affirmation should be given intentionally and deliberately, and not because we lack the energy, initiative or compassion to attempt an improvement.

This book presents a framework for ethical analysis that avoids both a simplistic reliance on party lines, and a paralysis in the face of daunting complexity. This framework offers an approach to identifying and understanding competing moral values, and to assessing their significance for particular public policy issues. The goal of this book is not to offer definite answers to all of the specific policy problems that bedevil us, but to improve the quality of our individual and collective deliberation about our responses to social problems. The aim is to establish a sure footing for ethical reflection about public policy decision making. "Public policy," simply stated, is whatever governments choose to do (or not to do). Public policies are the responses of government, through action or inaction, to social problems or to claims that are brought by the governed.

The essential question is, "What do we want government to do?" The answer is that we want government to provide benefits and prevent harms. We want government to provide those benefits and prevent those harms in an effective way. We want benefits and burdens to be distributed fairly. And, we want policies to be implemented in a manner that is respectful of persons. Further, we also want to ask, "What do we want government *not* to do?" We want government action to be limited to a sphere of influence that we consider legitimate.

From this statement, we can identify five benchmarks to be used in the moral evaluation of public policy: Benefit, Effectiveness, Fairness, Fidelity, and Legitimacy. I believe there is a broad-based national consensus that this short list describes what we as a nation want government to do. From sound bites in the media, through carefully crafted speeches to scholarly books and articles, these concerns appear again and again. If this perception is accurate, if there is widespread agreement that these statements reflect what we want government to do, then why is our national discussion about public policy marked by disagreement, acrimony, hostility, and deadlock? The divisions, and often stalemate, come when we provide content to these aspirations in particular cases, and especially when we have to establish priorities among these aspirations when they conflict with one another in specific policy choices. The rest of this book is devoted to a discussion of the content of, and the priorities among, these five benchmarks,

This conversation is fundamentally a moral conversation. Morality is inescapably at the heart of public policy choices. The formulation and evaluation of social policy is a matter of choosing among competing values, whether the decision makers recognize it or not. Policy considerations regularly entail examinations of clashes between such values as justice, liberty, security and equality. Some observers attempt to avoid this reality that policy choices are moral choices. These commentators fear that personal values will creep into policy analysis and decision making, and will thus displace an objectivity that they believe should guide policy making. As a result of this fear, discussions of the moral values that are embedded in policy proposals are often missing.

However, any attempt to engage in a "value-free" discussion of public policy will fail. We cannot make policy choices that are disconnected from value choices, and any effort to do so obscures the roles that beliefs and values do play. When we fail to acknowledge the role that morality plays, the result is the surreptitious and sometimes arbitrary introduction of beliefs and values into our discussions. Normative assumptions are not eliminated, they are just hidden from public scrutiny. The explicit consideration of values in policy discussions is the best protection against "creeping values." When the moral values are out in the open for everyone to see, it is then possible to subject them to careful scrutiny, a far better outcome than pretending that they do not exist.

Policy debates are moral debates, because policy making should be more than practical horse-trading. Ethics forces us to explore what *should* be done before we settle for what *can* be done. Ethical reflection leads us to look past how things are and are likely to be, and to consider how things ought to be. There is, of course, no moral responsibility to do that which is impossible, so adding a dose of ethics into the public policy discussion should not send us off on endless quixotic quests. Politics is still an art of the possible. Indeed, public policy discussions in the United States often move within relatively limited boundaries. These boundaries focus discussions on what is "doable" or what the country can or is willing to pay to solve a particular problem. A general consensus often exists that sets limits on the range of such policy debates, and these limits guide searches for answers along relatively well-established tracks. This self-imposed limitation on policy arguments grows out of a strong pragmatic element in the American public scene.

Pragmatism focuses on concerns of feasibility, practicality and possibility. Thus, many policy debates are limited by agreements, acknowledged or tacit, about what most of the American people want, what Congress would approve, what powerful constituencies would accept, or the amount of funding that is available. The strength of this pragmatic approach lies in the national cohesion it can foster and the efficiency it can bring to searches for solutions to social problems. But if this pragmatism fosters a climate in which agreements can be more easily reached, it may also blind us to possibilities for renewal and reform. It shackles the participants in the policy conversations, limiting their vision and preventing them from imagining all of the futures that might be.

Ethics is a challenge to pragmatic politics as it is often practiced. We should look beyond the walls of established convention, and not settle too quickly for what seems to be most feasible. When we accept a pragmatic alternative because it can be easily implemented, we ought to question whether we are accepting something less than the ideal, and we should be very clear about why we are accepting a compromise. If we don't lift our eyes higher, we may fool ourselves into thinking that today's feasible option is a permanently desirable option. Policy choices benefit from a full ethical deliberation that is not short-circuited by a pragmatic override. Honest, searching ethical discussions can illuminate options that have not previously fallen within the immediate general consensus. Such discussions may change the boundaries of the possible. What *can* be done is a function of social structures that have been created by people and that can be changed by people. When practicality does force us to do less than we want to do, we should be aware that we are doing less, we should know why we are doing less, and on occasion we should even do it with regret or anguish.

This book proposes a framework that incorporates both idealistic aspirations and pragmatic constraints. The aim is to foster a public discourse that is open, robust, and informed, which would lead to public decisions that are more firmly and openly grounded in the moral choices that are inevitably being made. The approach is holistic, in that it attempts to encompass all of the factors that should be taken into account in a moral assessment of policy—including principles or benchmarks that are often conflicting and contradictory. The purpose of the framework is to provide direction for analyzing responses to countless social problems, a blueprint for assessing public policy.

The core of the framework consists of the five principles of benefit, effectiveness, fairness, fidelity and legitimacy. These principles identify the values that should guide our evaluation of policies and policy proposals. *Benefit* and *Effectiveness* reflect our desires that policies produce benefits and avoid harms, and that they do so in an effective way. *Fairness* embodies our concern that public policies allocate burdens and benefits in a just manner. *Fidelity* gives voice to our sense that the government has certain obligations rooted in a respect for those who are affected by its actions. *Legitimacy* is the criterion for judging when the government should become the instrument for solving our social problems.

On the face of it, these principles seem unobjectionable. Yet, their meaning and significance are highly contested in the policy process, and each of them is subject to distortion. To mention just a few examples at this point: Benefit has been captured by a radical subjectivism that relies on "revealed preferences" to understand what is good. Effectiveness has been shrunk by an economic reductionism in which the only preferences that matter are economic. Fairness is weakened by an increasing polarization in the tension between liberty and equality. Fidelity is often ignored in a political climate which is short-sighted, temporally and spatially. Legitimacy has become little more than a grab bag of options that are used inconsistently, opportunistically, and hypocritically in pursuit of personal agendas.

This framework of five principles is offered to keep policy debates from becoming chaotic and directionless. However, presentations of theoretical frameworks that are divorced from concrete issues run the risk of becoming too abstract and meaningless. For this reason, examples will always be close at hand in the chapters that develop the five ethical benchmarks. These examples illustrate the significance of these principles, demonstrating the stakes involved and the consequences for applying these theoretical concepts in the real world. At the same time, the particular cases can be used to test the adequacy of the principles, giving the reader an opportunity to assess the framework in light of judgments about concrete issues.

Chapter 2 presents an introduction to ethics that is tailored to public policy discussions. This brief introduction is not meant to serve as a comprehensive look at the discipline of ethics.[1] The purpose of the chapter is simply to introduce the kinds of reasons that can be given for arguing that a public policy is morally desirable, and the chapter concludes with a fuller description of the five ethical benchmarks that provide the structure for the remainder of the book.

Chapters 3 through 7 explore the meaning and value of the principles of benefit, effectiveness, fairness, fidelity, and legitimacy. The working hypothesis of this book is that the ethical analysis of public policy issues can be usefully organized around this set of principles. As is emphasized later, these "principles" do not function in a mechanical way. My suggestion is *not* that these principles or rules should be applied to particular cases in order to produce logical conclusions. These principles, rather, are meant to identify factors that should be taken into account, concerns that should be given due consideration, matters that ought to be addressed when reflecting morally on a public policy option. They provide a framework within which moral problems can be identified, examined and resolved.

I have attempted to capture the tone of this kind of moral assessment by introducing the concept of the "benchmark." Benchmarks, in surveying, were fixed points left on a surveying line to provide points of reference at a later date. These benchmarks consisted of such things as cuts in trees and pegs driven into the ground. They came to refer more specifically to a surveyor's mark that was cut into some durable material, such as a rock or wall. The purpose of these wedge-shaped incisures (⑊) was to mark points in a level line that was used to determine altitudes. In the twenty-first century the term benchmark has come to refer to standards that are used to measure performance in a variety of activities, ranging from computer programs to national economies.

A key feature of the surveyors' benchmarks was their imprecision, due to the imperfection of the instruments and errors inherent in their use, as well as their movement over time. The nature of the surveyor's art is reflected in this textbook observation: "The best surveyor is not the one who makes the most precise measurements, but the one who is able to choose and apply the appropriate measure of precision requisite to the purpose."[2] The concepts introduced here are similarly imprecise, and our task of ethical assessment will be to apply these moral benchmarks in ways that are appropriate to different contexts. The benchmarks are offered as ingredients in a thoughtful analysis of public policy. When we praise someone as being thoughtful, we are not simply saying that she thinks a lot, but that she has a sense of what is important to think about. These principles identify things that are important to think about.

The eighth and final chapter draws these five disparate elements together into a cohesive approach to policy issues. The most interesting policy debates are those in which there is a conflict of values, in which, for example, a highly beneficial policy appears to violate notions of fairness, or is one that can only be implemented through shortchanging the demands of fidelity.

Complicating matters further is the reality that policies do not neatly yield yes-or-no answers to these principled questions. Actual policies or proposals will satisfy, or fail to satisfy, these moral standards to varying degrees; there will be degrees of effectiveness, degrees of fairness, and a sensitive ethical analysis must take this complexity into account. The purpose of Chapter 8 is to explore the relationships that exist among these principles and to make some observations about how we can assess the importance of these competing values in a meaningful way.

Notes

1   For examples of fuller explorations of the subject of ethics, see John Deigh, *An Introduction to Ethics* (Cambridge: Cambridge University Press, 2010); and Tom L. Beauchamp and James F. Childress, *Principles of Biomedical Ethics*, 7th ed. (New York: Oxford University Press, 2012).
2   Milton O. Schmidt and William Horace Rayner, *Fundamentals of Surveying*, 2nd ed. (New York: D. Van Nostrand Co., 1978), p. 8.

2 Ethical Discourse and Public Policy

Ethics is thinking about the question "What ought I to do?" Or, in the collective form in which the question is asked in the public policy context, "What should we do?" Ethics as a discipline is often divided into three branches—descriptive ethics, metaethics, and normative ethics. Descriptive ethics is an attempt to describe moral beliefs and actions as they exist, examining how people have answered the question, "What should we do?" Metaethics analyzes the meaning of ethical concepts, and studies the kinds of reasoning employed in arriving at answers to the question. Thus, for example, metaethics focuses on the meaning of such terms as "right" and "wrong." The focus of this book is on normative ethics, the third branch of the discipline. Persons engaged in normative ethics seek to provide answers to the question, "What should we do?"

We make hundreds of decisions every day. We are constantly making choices to act in one way or another, choices that are made in a taken-for-granted fashion. Our choices often come easily, without thought. We act on the basis of expectations that have been internalized, as we proceed through our everyday routine without serious reflection upon why we choose each of the things we do. From time to time, however, we find ourselves in a situation in which our choice does not come to us immediately. We encounter a set of circumstances that gives us pause, forces us to consider alternative courses of action or evaluate the correctness of the seemingly automatic choice. We stop and consciously ask the normative question: "What ought I to do?" When this happens, when we reflect on moral choices, we are "doing ethics."

Not all of our life's activities call for such reflection. We do not, for example, normally reflect on whether to breathe or not. This continuation of basic life-sustaining activities is a part of our actions that we take for granted. We do not stop and reflect upon what we should do about breathing. However, the circumstances are changed for someone who is terminally ill and is sustained by artificial ventilation devices. The routine nature of breathing is challenged in ways that force that person to view breathing in a new light. The normative question is then asked in a way that demands ethical reflection. Similarly, we are not usually called to think about morality as we choose a seat upon boarding a bus. In most cases we simply place our money in the collection box and move on to an empty seat without much more thought than noticing whether there is an acquaintance we wish to sit with or an empty seat for our shopping bag or briefcase. For Rosa Parks, however, choosing a seat on a bus became a choice that demanded ethical reflection. She was forced to make the decision about choosing a seat in a situation that did not yield a routine answer.

Thus, in one sense, the first ethical question is: "Is there a problem?" We usually pause to reflect ethically only if we have some clue that there is something problematic about our routine way of responding to the world. As a society, we begin to analyze public policies when the status quo doesn't work, or when we see that existing policies are taking us toward futures that we don't want. We may be presented with some information that we find troubling. We may encounter a situation that is so new, or that is so uncertain, that we aren't sure if our ordinary mode of action fits. We may find ourselves with conflicting responses about how to proceed or we may discover that other people are challenging our routine response. In these and other ways we are sent a message that there may be a problem, that we need to stop to determine whether there is a problem that should be addressed and, if so, to figure out how we should respond to that problem.

The very notion of "problem" is a value-based label. Situations become problematic when facts are viewed in the light of beliefs and values. For example, we may be presented with evidence that physicians are concentrated in urban areas and that 23 counties in a state do not have an obstetrician within their borders. But that situation is identified as a problem only when those data are viewed in light of certain moral convictions about health care, its distribution, and access to it by citizens. Similarly, information about pollution levels, extent of drug use, numbers of individuals without health insurance, or any other issue does not in itself identify a problem. A state of affairs is deemed to be a problem only when the judgment is made that the current state of affairs differs from what *ought* to be the case. And, of course, any statement about what ought to be the case, about what kind of society we should have, is based on ethical values.

Any particular situation presents a problem only in relation to a vision of what is good. A particular act becomes a problem only when judged by a standard of right action that requires different behavior. Therefore, our answer to the question—Is there a problem?—depends upon an ethical frame of reference. The purpose of this chapter is to look at some approaches, some ethical frames of reference, for identifying and solving moral problems.

Talking about Ethics

Is it possible to have a meaningful argument about ethical judgment? Consider this example, typical of illustrations that are often found in ethics textbooks:

Suppose that you are mountain climbing with your
closest friend, a person whom you admire and respect,
and from whom you have received many favors.
Suppose you lose your grip on a rope while he is
descending a sheer cliff. He falls. By the time
you reach him he is dying. In these dying moments
he asks that you make a promise to him, and you
agree. He reveals a great financial secret he has
been harboring. Through years of hard work and careful
investments he has hoarded a million dollars. He asks
you to deliver this money to an uncle. But you know
that this uncle is very rich. He not only doesn't need
the money but he pursues a lifestyle that leads you to
suspect he will squander the money. No one else knows
about either the promise or the secret cash. You believe
you can put the money to much better use by giving it
to charitable institutions. What do you do?

Is it possible to have a meaningful argument about what should be done in
such a case? Or is it just a matter of subjective individual preferences?

An assumption that underlies the discussion of ethics in this book is that
moral judgments are more than personal preferences, that reasons can be
given to support moral conclusions. Not everyone accepts this assumption.
There are those who believe that moral judgments are completely personal
and subjective and therefore are not amenable to rational analysis. They
believe that questions about whether a policy is good or just or equitable are
questions of personal taste that lie beyond the bounds of reasoned discourse.
An extreme example is emotivism, a philosophical view that ethical statements simply express emotional attitudes—a view that all moral judgments
are merely expressions of feelings or preferences. For some emotivists,
saying that killing is wrong is the same as saying "I don't like killing." The
moral judgment is only an expression of a personal attitude for which no
justification is required.

The contrary approach taken in this book is that moral judgments *can* be
argued about in a meaningful way. Our society's expectations about public
discourse concerning moral judgments presume such an approach. Mere
personal preferences do not require that reasons be given or that justifications be offered for those preferences. A selection of chocolate ice cream or
a positive emotional response to a piece of music does not require a reasoned
justification. But when someone makes a moral claim—for example, that
capital punishment is a good thing—we expect such a position to be justified by reasons. If someone were to take such a position as the claim that
capital punishment is a good thing, but yet did not offer any rationale to
support that position, we would dismiss such a person as not being seriously
engaged with the issue.

We do expect that value judgments will be based on reasons. We do believe that some justifications can be given that form a basis for evaluating those judgments. We act as though we can distinguish between good reasons and bad reasons for adopting a moral position. This book presents and examines the kinds of reasons that are used in meaningful conversations about ethical disagreement, moving us beyond the children on the playground who shout back and forth at each other "Is too!" and "Is not!"

The claim that we can have meaningful conversations about moral judgments does not mean that moral positions can be proven empirically, like scientific proofs. Rather, moral discourse has its own kind of rationality and its own kind of validation. The moral justifications that we adopt or accept are not so much "true" as they are powerful, convincing or persuasive. The standard for judgment is not verification (verus, the true in Latin), but rather validity (*validus*, the strong, powerful, mighty, influential).[1] The concept of truth does apply to some of the premises of moral arguments—for example, the understanding of the facts of a situation—but it does not apply to the arguments themselves. Arguments are judged according to their cogency. A cogent argument is one that is convincing or believable by virtue of its clear, forceful and incisive nature.

In the pages that follow, I briefly describe some of the kinds of reasons that have been given to support and justify ethical positions. These descriptions illustrate what count as good reasons for ethical conclusions in three prominent ethical traditions.[2] I first describe two approaches that are grounded in the great classical traditions that have been given labels derived from the Greek words for end or purpose, and for duty or obligation: teleology and deontology, respectively. Following that discussion is an introduction to a third approach that has gained more attention in recent decades, an ethics of response that attends to matters not fully treated in the two traditional approaches. This chapter concludes with an elaboration of the five ethical benchmarks that can guide discussion of public policy issues, and that serve as the framework for the remainder of the book.

Achieving Results

One type of ethics focuses on consequences. A teleological approach to ethics judges human action by the results that our acts produce. The appeal is to the value of the ends that flow from particular choices. Questions of morality are seen as largely questions of consequences. Ethical reflection upon whether a public policy is right or wrong centers on an analysis of the results produced by that policy. Policy is analyzed in terms of the good (and bad) consequences that flow from that policy, especially as those results are compared to the consequences of other available alternatives. The dictum that "the ends justify the means" is an expression of this perspective on morality.

A teleological approach to the illustration of the mountain climber who made a promise to deliver his deceased friend's money to a high-living uncle would look at the consequences that would follow from the possible options. Is giving the money to the uncle, in fact, the course of action that would produce the best results? A teleological analysis might lead the mountain climber to donate the money to charity, arguing that since no one else knows of the promise, no negative result would follow from breaking that promise. His decision would depend upon an analysis of the consequences of each choice.

In our daily lives, we often employ this kind of means-and-ends reasoning. We take medication in order to rid our bodies of infection; we canvas door-to-door to promote a desired election result. As a nation we vaccinate children to prevent epidemics and we build missiles to deter would-be aggressors. In each case, the worth of an act—and of a policy—lies in the results it produces.

Utilitarianism is the most widely practiced form of consequentialism, especially in the world of public policy analysis. According to the utilitarian standard, an act is right if it produces the greatest possible balance of good consequences compared to bad consequences. The goal is to maximize benefit and minimize harm. For John Stuart Mill, the best known of the early utilitarians,[3] the principle of utility equated happiness with benefit, and pain with harm, so that actions were judged by the net happiness or pleasure they produced.

Not all utilitarians have agreed with Mill that happiness or pleasure is the ultimate good that should inform our ethical calculations. Others have suggested that health or wisdom, for example, are also goods that should be valued in this way. The lack of consensus about what benefit should mean has led to the development of two different approaches to utilitarianism: welfare-based utilitarianism and preference-based utilitarianism.

Welfare-based utilitarianism begins with judgments about goods, about the things that constitute human well-being—such as life, health or financial wealth. Anyone who makes utilitarian judgments identifies the goods that enhance our welfare, and then evaluates various courses of action in terms of their projected ability to maximize these goods. Traditionally, discussions about the good that we should pursue were dominated by clergymen, philosophers, or kings. The problem is that, even after centuries of debate, there is often disagreement about what constitutes human welfare. Some measure the good life in terms of personal freedom, others in terms of service to others, and still others in terms of happiness or financial well-being. This lack of consensus has led many present-day utilitarians to reject this welfare-based utilitarianism and to use instead a standard of personal preferences.

In preference-based utilitarianism, benefit is defined to be whatever people want; maximizing the beneficial consequences for a person means acting so as to give her the most of what she desires. This approach avoids the interminable debates about what is truly good or beneficial. Instead, benefit is defined as the satisfaction of the preferences of a chosen group of people. Policies are evaluated by the degree to which they give people what they want. The preference-based approach, however, does raise the issue of whether there are some preferences that should not be honored because they are immoral or unjust. If a group of citizens desires the subjugation of another race, for example, that hardly seems like a preference that should be honored in a utilitarian calculation. But as soon as any preferences are deemed to be out of bounds, judgments are being made through a process that deviates from a purely preference-based approach.

Utilitarians can also be divided in another way, into act utilitarians and rule utilitarians. An act utilitarian argues that a person should perform the act that leads to the greatest good for the greatest number of people in each and every situation. An act utilitarian considers rules such as "You ought to keep promises" as little more than summaries of good decisions made in the past. Therefore, he would feel obligated to violate such a guideline in any set of circumstances in which the greatest good for the greatest number would result from breaking a promise. In each and every case, the decision maker is obligated to make a fresh calculation about whether moral norms that have been valid in the past have any weight in the new situation.

Rule utilitarians, on the other hand, believe that rules such as "You ought to keep promises" have more moral weight. A rule utilitarian asks, "What would happen if everyone were to act in a particular way in such cases?" For her, rules should be followed if they are the rules that would produce the greatest good for the greatest number when they are consistently followed. Thus, a utilitarian justification exists for the rule. For rule utilitarians, the willingness of act utilitarians to violate such rules in particular cases destroys the effectiveness of the rules, leading to a less beneficial future in the long run.

The argument between act utilitarians and rule utilitarians turns on the issue of which approach would actually produce the most net benefit when all of the consequences are taken into account. The rule utilitarian wins if the case-by-case exceptions to moral rules advocated by the act utilitarian would either lead to a breakdown in the effectiveness of moral systems, or result in individuals making too many errors in calculating net benefit. The act utilitarian wins if individual judgments in particular cases would produce a greater good than would be produced by following general rules. Re-visiting the mountain climbing illustration, the rule utilitarian might focus on the utility of following a rule that one should keep promises while the act utilitarian would attempt to calculate the consequences of the options available in this specific situation for all affected parties.

Obeying Rules

Historically, the primary competitor to consequentialist ethics has been deontological ethics. For the deontologist, there are considerations that should govern moral choice other than the consequences of actions. It is possible for an act to be morally right even if it does not produce the greatest net balance of good. In this view, morality is not a matter of producing good results, but of meeting obligations that are related to the nature of the actions themselves, rather than their results. Religious traditions give us examples of this approach to making moral choices. The Ten Commandments are understood by many to be rules that should be followed, not because they produce good results but because they are commanded by God. Sharia law similarly offers a set of rules to be obeyed. Religious codes of conduct are not open to validation by an assessment of the consequences of abiding by those codes. Rather, their validity rests in their source. Not all non-consequentialist ethical systems are religious, as some of them rest instead on intuition (which finds certain truths to be "self-evident"), or human reason.

Immanuel Kant was an eighteenth-century philosopher whose writings present perhaps the most important statement of a consistent non-consequentialist ethic. He attempted to describe moral principles that can be used to judge whether actions are right or wrong, and for him such moral rules can be known only through the exercise of reason. Reason alone, not observations of consequences, can reveal the basic moral principles that should guide the action of all persons.

The fundamental principle for Kant was his Categorical Imperative: We should always act in such a way that we can will that the principle that directs the act would become a universal law. This principle is categorical—in that it admits of no exceptions regardless of other considerations—and it is an imperative—in that it commands certain moral action. This first statement of the Categorical Imperative is a generalization at a fairly abstract level. Kant provides another formulation of the Categorical Imperative that provides more substance to this concept: rational beings (humans) should always be treated as ends in themselves and never only as means to ends. This formulation, which is the formulation most immediately applicable in modern policy discussions, demands that a person never treat others purely as a means to achieving one's own ends.

Policies that require informed consent are among the most obvious applications of this moral principle. The principle, for example, prohibits the use of uninformed, non-consenting persons as subjects in medical experimentation, regardless of the perceived benefits of the results to others. President Clinton adhered to this principle when he established new regulations that prohibited government-financed secret experiments using radioactive, chemical or other dangerous materials on unknowing human subjects.

The feature common to all types of non-consequentialism is that matters of right and wrong are judged by standards other than the results that are produced by certain actions. In each case there is something about the character of a behavior, other than its consequences, that provides a basis for ethical evaluation. Returning to our mountain climbing illustration, a deontologist's decision will depend on the principles or rules he believes he is obligated to follow. One of these non–consequentialist rules could be that we should keep promises. A deontologist who is bound by this rule would find that our mountain climber should keep the promise and give the money to the uncle even though that would not be the "best" use to which the money could be put.

Deontological positions have not gone unchallenged. Given the fact that there are differing, conflicting versions of non–consequentialist rules that we should follow, what basis other than increasing welfare do we have for choosing among them? How do we decide among the competing sources of obligation such as reason, tradition, or divine revelation? Further, utilitarians can mount a serious challenge to this entire approach: Are not result-oriented considerations covertly the basis of even the most rigidly deontological systems, such as Kant's? Take the example of a promise that is a lie. True enough, if everyone made lying promises as a matter of course the institution of promising would self-destruct. But is that a "reasonable" grounding of the rule that prohibits lying promises, or does a prohibition of lying ultimately rely on a consequentialist argument? That consequentialist argument would be that the result of the destruction of the institution of promising would be the creation of a world without reliable promises, and that is a consequence we want to avoid. Finally, which approach best fits our moral experience? Particularly in the world of public policy, do we aspire to a morality based on such rules or do we aspire to a public morality that has public benefit as its focus? These and other questions can be explored more fully in the context of subsequent chapters, especially those on Fairness and Fidelity.

Responding to Others

Many ethicists are not satisfied with the either/or choice they have been given in the traditional achieving results vs. obeying rules debate. This dissatisfaction lies not in a lack of appreciation for the value in either approach, but in a sense that they both tell only part of the story, that each approach oversimplifies the very complex process through which we convert values into deeds and policies. William Frankena, for example, has written the book *Ethics*, the book that may have been used more than any other to introduce students to ethics. He shows his own dissatisfaction with the either/or choice by proposing a "mixed deontological theory."[4] He says this theory takes into account both the pursuit of certain results (maximizing the balance of good over evil in the world) and adherence to certain deontological principles (such as justice, and perhaps keeping promises). The problem with any such mixed system is deciding when one approach overrides the other. When *do* the ends justify the means? When do they not? When does keeping a promise take priority over maximizing results? Frankena does not offer any suggestions to help his readers find the answers to such questions.

A more fundamental dissatisfaction with the teleological and deontological modes was experienced by Albert Jonsen and Stephen Toulmin. They
have described an alternative approach to ethics that grew out of their experience with the National Commission for the Protection of Human Subjects
of Biomedical and Behavioral Research, an experience that led them to
write *The Abuse of Casuistry*. The commission's charge was to review federal
research regulations that protect the "rights and welfare" of research subjects
in biomedical and behavioral investigations. This task included the development of general statements of ethical principles that would serve as guides in
the conduct of biomedical and behavioral research.

The eleven commissioners possessed widely varying backgrounds and
interests. The diversity of the commission—in terms of gender, race,
religion, profession, philosophical and political commitments—provided
ample grounds for skepticism about the possibility that the commission
could forge agreement on general principles or on the application of principles to particular problems. All the more striking, then, were Jonsen's
and Toulmin's observations that the commission members were largely in
agreement about particular practical recommendations. They observed that
"[s]erious differences of opinion began to appear only when individual
commissioners went beyond the stage of formulating practical proposals and
explained their individual *reasons* for participating in the collective recommendations."[5] That is, they often agreed on everything except *why* they
agreed.

These commissioners could not reach a consensus about whether they
should take a teleological or a deontological approach. They were not able
to devise a set of mutually shared systematic general principles that would
direct their moral inquiry, but they were able to find some consensus in
their responses to specific cases. For Jonsen and Toulmin, this experience
suggested that abstract theoretical generalizations are afterthoughts or
methodological window-dressing that develops after the actual work of
moral analysis has already been done. These types of experiences have led
some ethicists to develop understandings of moral decision making that are
more focused on particular cases or relationships.

It is not necessary to completely reject the grand theories of deontology
and teleology in order to develop a model that recognizes their limitations
and that more fully reflects the realities of human moral decision making.
One such model for ethics is the ethics of response developed by H. Richard
Niebuhr in *The Responsible Self*.[6] The core of Niebuhr's ethic is the image
of the person-as-responder, which he contrasts with the teleological person-
as-maker and the deontological person-as-citizen. Understanding persons as
responders means that human actions are viewed primarily as neither
attempts to achieve results nor efforts to follow rules. Rather, they are
viewed essentially as responses. This understanding of human action is
rooted in the experience of persons being engaged in dialogue—answering
questions, replying to orders, meeting challenges—of persons acting in

response to actions upon themselves. Actions are judged neither by achievement of results nor adherence to rules but by how appropriate those actions are, by how well they fit in the context in which a person is acting. When persons act appropriately in this sense, they are being responsible.

Carol Gilligan has described this meaning of responsibility as acting responsively in relationships.[7] She emphasizes that the self exists in relationship to others and that the reference points for our moral judgments are those relationships. This morality of response focuses on our situatedness, our interdependence, our connectedness with one another. This emphasis can be contrasted with traditional teleological and deontological approaches that view individuals principally as independent and separate, and that stress neutral rules and principles. A particular type of response ethics, an ethics of care, has grown out of this pioneering work done by Gilligan. An ethics of care focuses on relationships, on an awareness of the features of a particular situation, a sympathetic identification with all persons in the situation, and a concern for networks of care.[8] This conception of ethics recasts the nature of our moral obligations toward others. The distinctiveness of this approach can be seen, for example, by considering the difference between the honored statement that "all men are created equal . . . with certain unalienable rights" and a possible alternate formulation: "all persons are created interdependent with mutual responsibility to aid others."[9]

In an ethics of response, persons are not viewed as autonomous individuals making choices about which principles to follow (whether results-oriented or rule-based). The response approach to ethics is one in which particular judgments precede principles or, more precisely, in which we continually move back and forth between general principles and judgments in specific cases. We modify our understanding of principles to fit our concrete judgments, and we alter our view of cases to fit our principles. Moral intuition is understood not as a glimpse of some transcendent morality but as reflective discernment rooted in shared values.

"Reflective equilibrium" is the label John Rawls has given to this movement between principles and specific judgments.[10] We shuttle back and forth between judgments in specific cases and our general principles, seeking to find a balance between the two. Often they will fit neatly together; other times we find some dissonance, even outright conflict, between what we think we believe and what we think is right in a particular instance. On those occasions we reflect on the differences and often make an adjustment on one side or other. In recent decades, for example, most Americans have changed their general beliefs about how gays and lesbians should be treated. Typically the change in principles has come when they discovered that their principles called for treatment that just wasn't right when it was applied to people they knew—often their children, brothers and sisters. On the other hand, continued reflection on principles can alter initial judgments about a specific case, as has occurred for many Americans in recent years as support has waned for affirmative action quotas in college admissions. The reflective search for equilibrium is a life-long project, a process that does not hold the promise of any final resting place.

Returning to the mountain climbing illustration, a person engaged in a response ethics type of reflection might well think about the rule that promises should be kept and also project the consequences that would flow from alternative uses of the money. But such a person would also reflect on other realities, such as: the character of the relationship that existed between him and his friend, including the value traditions they shared and the wisdom those traditions might bring to this dilemma; the extent to which the request was consistent with a long life of value commitments and priorities; the web of relationships that constitute his life and the moral expectations of those with whom he is most meaningfully connected. Reflection on the features of this particular case could lead to new understandings about the principles that promises should be kept, or that the use of goods should be maximized. In the end, the decision would rest not on applying a rule or calculating a result, but responding to the totality of the circumstances.

Five Benchmarks

I am proposing that the ethical evaluation of public policies be organized around five ethical benchmarks. The principles offered in this book identify the kinds of reasons that can be given in support of, or in criticism of public policies. The benchmarks identify considerations to be taken into account. They are topics for attention, items for discussion, factors to be included in the analysis. They point to the kinds of questions that need to be asked, rather than providing the answers to the questions. In a pluralistic society different traditions will bring different significance and substance to each of these considerations. An important aspect of the policy-making task is to understand the shifting, evolving content of these principles, and the various ways they have functioned in our public discourse.

Developing a list of moral principles does not eliminate a place for individual moral assessment. Two persons employing the same benchmarks can come to different conclusions about a given case (in the same way that persons using different approaches can come to similar conclusions). Principled arguments can take us a long way toward reaching a moral decision, but finally, at some point, we must rely on our individual judgments. The use of principles to fashion ethical arguments can structure our conversations in ways that make clear the role these individual judgments play in our moral decision making. But eventually such elements—captured by such labels as intuition, seasoned judgment or moral discernment—are the features of ethical reflection that make moral choice a uniquely personal enterprise.

These five benchmarks have emerged from my examination of public policy discourse and the ethical literature on normative decision making. An analysis of policy discourse has revealed these principles as elements that regularly appear in public debates and in the scholarly literature. These are the themes that recur in important ways in the rhetoric used in values-related policy debates. Similarly, the concerns embodied in these five principles address the major themes that philosophers and ethicists have raised in their discussions of the norms that inform moral choice. I have found this format to be useful in organizing my thinking about the moral analysis of public policy. My hope is that others will find them similarly helpful.

What should we be concerned about when we are making moral assessments of government policies and actions? *We should be concerned that benefits are provided (or harms avoided), that those benefits are provided and harms are avoided in an effective way, that burdens and benefits are distributed fairly, and that the policies that serve these concerns are implemented in a manner that is respectful of persons.* In this summary statement we recognize the values of Benefit, Effectiveness, Fairness and Fidelity. The fifth: Not every problem should be the government's problem—that is, we are concerned about the Legitimacy of government action.

These five principles are embedded in the ethical theories of teleology, deontology, and response ethics that were described earlier. *Benefit* and *Effectiveness* are about achieving results. A concern with ends looks to harms and benefits to justify ethical decisions. A full consideration of ends looks not only at the direct product of policies—the harms that are avoided or the benefits that are secured—but also at the costs entailed in avoiding those harms or securing those benefits.

Critics of teleology most often criticize this approach on two grounds: (1) it does not adequately take into account how benefits are distributed and costs are allocated, and (2) it does not adequately recognize moral obligations that arise in such actions as making promises, or entering into contracts, or in relationships that otherwise create special responsibilities to others. Deontological ethics has often moved persons away from the single-minded pursuit of maximizing benefits by calling attention to the principle of *Fairness*: persons should get what they deserve, goods and services should be justly distributed, particular individuals and groups should not bear an unfair burden in the implementation of a public policy, like cases should be treated alike. Such standards focus not on aggregate results but the way results are distributed among various persons and constituencies. The language of rights and entitlements has also been used to describe fair treatment of individuals (they have a right to certain goods or services; they are entitled to those things they deserve). In addition, deontologists have often used standards such as "Tell the Truth" or "Keep Promises." The principle of *Fidelity* incorporates these kinds of concerns, concerns that are sometimes better captured by the relational focus of a response ethics than by the rules created by deontologists.

More broadly, an ethics of response recognizes an appropriate place for achieving results and obeying rules. Ethical reflection appropriately responds to all features of our moral lives—the goals we pursue, the rules we obey, and the relationships we forge. A response ethics also pays special attention to the context in which a response is elicited, looking for a fit between the action in question and the situation involved. In the case of public policy a primary feature of that context is the social institution being expected to act: government. A response that is appropriate for a family, or a church, or a business will not always constitute an appropriate response for the government. Thus, we consider the principle of *Legitimacy* because we realize that a potential response by the government may not be desirable even if it appears to pass the test of the other four principles.

Benefit

Benefit is the first principle to be examined. We want public policies that produce good results, or at least prevent bad ones. Defining what is beneficial, however, can be a complex process, especially in a community in which different people have very different views about the nature of a good society. How do we determine which results are good ones and how do we assign priority to competing goods? For example, a general agreement exists that providing federal funding for abortions would result in increased access to abortions for poor women. Most of those in favor of federal funding for abortions view such a consequence as a benefit; most of those opposed to such funding do not. How do we decide which view is correct? Funding by the National Endowment for the Arts results in the creation of artistic works that some find offensive. Sometimes, these are works that would never have been created if the artists had been forced to rely on the market place for support. Opinions vary about whether this funding, which results in the production of this art, provides a benefit.

Identification of the benefit that is being sought affects choice among policy options. As President George W. Bush and the nation attempted to formulate a policy to guide action against Saddam Hussein's Iraq, various benefits to be secured were identified. Among these were: (1) punishing the perpetrators of the 9/11 attack on America; (2) protecting the United States from Iraq's weapons of mass destruction; (3) destroying safe havens for terrorists and deterring future terrorist attacks; (4) protecting Iraq's neighbors from the military threat posed by that country; (5) liberating the Iraqi people from the rule of a brutal dictator; (6) creating a democracy in the Middle East that would spread freedom throughout the region; (7) punishing the regime that had violated U.N. resolutions; and (8) furthering American economic interests in the region.

In that debate, an individual's view of these various proffered benefits affected her decisions about which policy choices were appropriate. Some commentators viewed certain of these potential Iraq War benefits as illegitimate policy objectives for the United States. For others, the effectiveness with which some of these benefits could be achieved was a concern. There was considerable debate about whether deposing Hussein and trying to create a democracy in Iraq would be beneficial at all. And there remained the extremely complicated task of assigning weight and priority to this multitude of identified benefits, as the pursuit of some benefits would not necessarily lead to the same policy choices as the pursuit of others.[11]

The chapter on benefit will take up these questions: What is a benefit? How do we choose among competing benefits? There exists a particularly strong pull in a democracy toward relying on citizen preference as the means for answering these kinds of questions. Is this an acceptable approach? If not, what are our alternatives?

Effectiveness

Effectiveness is closely related to, if not inseparable from, Benefit. We want policies that produce benefits and avoid harms, and we want them to do so effectively. Those who govern have an obligation to use resources efficiently. Measurements of effectiveness typically focus on dollars, although broader conceptions of this benchmark also include such resources as time, energy, and opportunity. Cost-benefit analysis, cost-effectiveness analysis, and risk assessment are primary tools used by policy analysts in their efforts to assess how well a policy provides the desired results. These assessments inevitably raise questions about the valuing of various costs and benefits, as well as about which costs and benefits should be included in the evaluation.

We can find consensus that many results are beneficial—e.g., most of us would agree that saving lives through the prevention of premature illness and death is a benefit. The effectiveness criterion focuses not on whether this result is truly a benefit, but on the effectiveness of a particular policy as a means of achieving that benefit. Evaluating policies in light of effectiveness involves not only the results being produced, but the utilization of government resources in producing those results. For example, a controversy arose concerning enforcement of the federal Controlled Substances Act, when an increasing number of states were passing statutes that authorized the use of marijuana for medical purposes. On October 19, 2009, the U.S. Deputy Attorney General David W. Ogden issued a Department of Justice memorandum to all United States Attorneys to provide clarity and guidance to federal prosecutors.

He wrote that the memorandum was intended solely as "a guide to the exercise of investigative and prosecutorial discretion and as guidance on resource allocation and federal priorities." The memo recommends that patients using medical cannabis products in accordance with state laws should not be prosecuted. Such prosecutions, Ogden concluded, would likely be "an inefficient use of limited federal resources." This recommendation did not change federal law. It did not change the government's position, articulated by the Food and Drug Administration, that marijuana had no accepted value in the treatment of any disease. Rather, this policy on enforcement reflected the judgment that in some instances the prosecution of drug cases was not an effective use of government resources.

Concerns for effectiveness range beyond a straightforward cost-benefit analysis, to include such questions as: How should we handle the uncertainty of projections of costs and benefits for proposed policies? Can the resources that are required to implement one policy be used more effectively to solve other problems elsewhere in the community? Does the policy create new problems that should be weighed in the balance? How do we value a human life? How do we measure the benefit of a childhood free from smallpox, a 20 percent reduction in respiratory disease due to a reduction in pollution, an education enriched by music and art classes, or the dignity that comes with protection from discrimination? At the heart of the effectiveness inquiry is a trade-off between seemingly incommensurable benefits and costs, and making such tradeoffs is a profoundly moral activity.

Fairness

The benchmark of Fairness embodies the conviction that people should get what they deserve. Fairness in the criminal justice system means, among other things, that the innocent are acquitted, the guilty are punished, and the punishment inflicted is comparable to that received by other similarly situated individuals. More broadly, fairness dictates that burdens and benefits be allocated in a just manner. We believe that we should pay attention to how a government distributes goods and services and rewards, as well as how it allocates risks and burdens.

Different guidelines for achieving fairness, however, yield different results. For example, three standards that are used as a basis for distribution are equal shares, individual contribution, and need. Current policy regarding elementary education begins with an equal shares concept of distribution. The starting assumption is that the government should provide equal educational opportunity, an assumption that is reinforced by court decisions striking down school funding schemes that allocate more money for some local school districts than others in the same state. An equal shares model also undergirds our sense of what is fair in the distribution of fire protection and other essential services.

A different approach has been deemed to be fair, however, when setting up policy regarding the distribution of social security benefits. The beginning point here has not been equal shares, but individual contribution. Social benefits are not paid equally to all citizens at a certain age, but to those who have paid into the system for a specified number of quarters. And, to a certain extent, the amount that one receives is related to the amount one has contributed. Similarly, it is considered to be fair that extraordinary financial support for college education is provided through the G.I. Bill in response to the contribution that veterans have made to the well-being of the nation.

Yet another basis for distributing benefits is need. Within the overall Social Security system is the Supplemental Security Income program, providing assistance to those who need it because of disability. The food stamp program is another example of a distribution of benefits based on need. An equal amount of food stamps is not given to all citizens, only to those who need them. Some citizens are eligible for a variety of other benefits, such as Medicaid and FEMA grants, as a result of need-based determinations. Equal shares, individual contribution and need are only three of the many standards that are used to assess the fairness of policies that allocate benefits and services. Deciding which standard should be used in particular cases is at the core of some of our most heated debates about public policy.

Fidelity

The principle of Fidelity measures the extent to which a government meets obligations that are based on a respect for persons. The government should keep its promises, fulfill its contracts, and honor the commitments it has made. And those who govern should make and implement policy in a manner that is consistent with the legitimate expectations of those who are governed. Fidelity emphasizes a governmental obligation to respect the dignity of each person, a respect that is rooted in an understanding that individuals should not be treated merely as instruments in the pursuit of policy goals.

Ohio governor Ted Strickland was speaking about a commitment to fidelity in the spring of 2007 when he expressed his concern about the treatment of the men and women in the Ohio National Guard units who were being called up for the second time in two years: "The Government is not keeping faith with these men and women." Major General Gus L. Hargett, commander of the Tennessee National Guard, spoke from this same sense of obligation when he voiced a similar sentiment four years earlier: "We owe it to our soldiers, our families, and the employers of our National Guard troops to provide a predictable frame for deployments." The language used in both of these cases is about the government acting faithfully because of what it owes certain citizens.

Other types of obligations are created by specific government actions: governments sign contracts and enter into employment agreements. Commitments are also made through legislative actions, such as the "promise" made in 1982 that the government would find a place to safely store thousands of tons of highly radioactive waste from civilian power plants by February 1, 1998—a promise that a federal court reaffirmed created an obligation on the part of the Energy Department to accept used reactor fuel rods. With the promise still unfulfilled in August, 2012, the Nuclear Regulatory Commission stopped issuing licenses for nuclear power plants. The series of treaties signed by Native American tribes and the U.S. Government embody another set of commitments, commitments that were, on the whole, not kept.

Another expectation we have of government is that we will live under a system of laws that is reasonable, open and transparent. This expectation would rule out of bounds behavior such as that of Roman Emperor Caligula, who was said to have written his laws in very small characters and hung them high up on pillars so that they could not be read by citizens—although we've been told that federal regulations governing the boarding of an airplane by a passenger who does not have a picture identification are "secret."

All of these various senses of government obligation reflect the need for governors to respect those that are governed, to keep faith with the people. This benchmark of fidelity introduces an element into policy deliberations that is not accounted for by cost-benefit calculations or by certain concepts of justice and fairness. Policies that meet the tests (to one degree or another) of Benefit, Effectiveness and even Fairness may fail on this criterion—one that is especially important in a democratic society. The principle of Fidelity focuses on a government's respect for its citizens in the implementation and enforcement of policy—including the government's obligation to tell the truth, to avoid deception, to honor contracts and uphold commitments and keep promises, and to maintain the rules upon which people have relied.

Legitimacy

Legitimacy is a benchmark grounded in the assumption that there are some moral values that the government should enforce and there are other moral values that the government should not enforce. The question is when a problem is fair game for public policy. The killing of human beings is a moral problem that we have deemed to be an appropriate matter for governmental action. On the other hand, a parent's violation of a promise to a child to buy a bicycle is not normally the kind of matter that warrants governmental intervention. There is a consensus that the government should address the need for education for all citizens, but not the need for designer jeans—and the need for preventive health care currently falls some place in between these two topics in our national conversation. The justices on the United States Supreme Court have expressed conflicting views about whether it is a legitimate exercise of governmental power to prohibit "intimate sexual conduct" in private between consenting adults of the same gender.

If it is legitimate to implement public policies to address some problems, but not all problems, how do we decide which are legitimate matters for state regulation and which are not? The answers to this question are related to our value-laden views about the proper nature and role of the state, our assessment of human nature, and our view of the kind of community we desire.

Appeals to Emotion

These five benchmarks identify the kinds of reasons that can be given in support of policy positions. But the arguments that are often successful are not necessarily those that do the best job of satisfying these principles. We can hope that argumentation that is morally cohesive and rationally defensible will be convincing, but in the real world rational arguments sometimes fail to persuade while irrational forays that are little more than appeals to emotion sometimes succeed. Emotional appeals have played major roles in our public policy discourse about a variety of topics, such as abortion, affirmative action, the Iraq War, immigration, health care reform, and social service entitlements. Do appeals to emotion have a legitimate place in a debate about public policy? Some observers believe that reasoning by emotion entails logical fallacies and leads to bad decision making. According to this view, an argument based on feelings may be effective in the real world, but the fact that emotional appeals are effective is unfortunate and interferes with reaching correct public policy decisions.

I want to argue, however, in favor of an appropriate role for appeals to emotion in ethical debates about public policy matters. Emotional connections are inevitably a part of who we are, and they will invariably influence the ethical arguments we make. If we try to ignore this affective dimension of ourselves, then feelings will be smuggled into policy discussions—unacknowledged, unexamined, and unchallenged. Some argue that emotional exchanges damage the public debate. But if the power and influence of emotion is hidden, we face the even larger danger of subverting the kind of open, public debate that is so important to policy making in a democracy. The answer is not to deny a role for feelings in policy discussions, but to discipline our reliance on emotional appeals.

One model for bringing discipline to the use of emotions is to acknowledge a role for emotions in the decision making process, but only as feelings are constantly monitored and directed by reason. This is a model in which reason disciplines emotion, in which emotions are always subordinated to reason. Feelings are controlled by reason and are valid only when they are justified on independent reasonable grounds. According to this view, appeals to passion and feelings are seen as legitimate ways to motivate people to act, but there is no role for emotions to play in directing us to the correct action. Feelings are allowed to help us move from thought to action, within reason, but they are not viewed as having a proper role in determining the direction that action should take. If an emotional response matches the reasonable response then it is valid; if it is contrary to reasonable analysis, it is inappropriate. Therefore, there is no independent contribution that feelings can make in determining the appropriate content of public policy. This use of the concept of discipline is precisely what I *do not* have in mind.

The word "discipline" has two very different meanings. One is the restricting and confining notion that has just been illustrated. Discipline in this first sense involves limitations: soldiers are confined to quarters or restricted to base; children are put in "time out" or grounded; employees lose privileges, citizens forfeit entitlements, leaders suffer loss of esteem. When we think about disciplining emotions in this sense, we are thinking about restricting the range of emotions, eliminating emotional considerations from certain kinds of discourse, discounting the value of affective appeals in making policy decisions.

However, "discipline" also has a second meaning that needs to be brought to emotions and policy debates—an expanding and enabling notion. Athletes discipline their bodies, not to restrict their possibilities but to expand them. Military discipline, in this sense, entails not sending soldiers to the brig but training them in a way that increases their capability. The goal of this kind of discipline is to enhance, expand, and increase—to extend the reach of the subject.

Disciplining emotions in this sense means forcing an accounting for all relevant affective connections, not just those that come to mind quickly and easily. This discipline means turning affective sensibilities to a wide variety of subjects, to all of those subjects with whom we have some connection. This enhancement of our emotional capacity requires a discipline similar to that of the long distance runner who forces herself through her daily paces. It entails a pushing and stretching of ourselves so that we recognize and take account of a host of attachments that can lay claim to our emotions.

We should care about many different things and many different people. A deliberate effort to expand the scope of our caring yields a different kind of response. This approach does not eliminate emotion or sever connections. Rather it opens us up to a wider range of connections. A recognition of and a response to all of the emotional pulls and tugs that come our way will provide a discipline that will carry us beyond the hottest, most narrow impulses.

This second kind of disciplined emotions can be illustrated by looking at the debate on deficit reduction in recent decades. The American public was slow to adopt policies that reduced the size of the federal government deficit. For years, efforts by many economists and policy analysts to persuade citizens and legislators that meaningful steps should be taken to reduce the ever-increasing deficit were largely ineffective. With the 1992 presidential campaign, however, the ground began to shift. It became increasingly feasible, and even popular, to carry the banner of deficit reduction in a serious way. The depth of the public's conviction that it was time for a change was revealed not only in the voter support for Ross Perot, but also in the executive and legislative action in the first months of the Clinton administration.

Why did the argument that the deficit should be reduced become a more persuasive one? The cause of deficit reduction did not carry the day as long as the message was simply an economic one that such a large and increasing debt load was bad for the nation's economy. Neither did the moral judgment that deficit budgets were bad in themselves (in the same way that failing to balance your personal checking account was bad) have much of an impact. On the spending side, such arguments carried little weight when put up against the emotional commitments of bleeding-heart liberals who were still trying to build a great society, or of super-patriotic conservatives who were battling evil empires around the globe. Similarly, the suggestion that spending should be cut barely moved family members whose parents and grandparents depended on Social Security and Medicare to maintain their standard of living. On the taxing side, the fact that comparative financial analyses showed that, relatively speaking, we were *not* an over-taxed nation did not persuade taxpayers who had their own personal reasons for wanting to enforce presidential promises of no new taxes.

Financial analysis, economic projections and philosophical deduction alone did not persuade American citizens and legislators that dramatic action was needed to reduce the deficit. The debate shifted in the 1992 presidential campaign when the facts were personified and an emotional consideration became the focus of the argument. Suddenly it was not just economics but a new framing of the issue: the pattern of government financing was robbing our children and grandchildren of their future. Those being harmed were no longer nameless, faceless "future generations." They were our kids, and there are few sentimental connections that can compete with the emotional ties of parents and children. The debate shifted when the populace embraced this emotional attachment, an attachment that had been relegated to the shadows while the spotlight had been on national defense, the poor, the elderly, or our own pocketbooks.

The days of federal budget surpluses receded, of course, as new emotion-laden arguments came to the fore early in the twenty-first century. The fear generated by the 9/11 attacks, and seven years later by an economy in free fall, led to a return to deficit spending. In the absence of a community commitment to shared sacrifice that might have supported increased taxes or spending reductions in other areas, "tax and spend" was replaced by "borrow and spend" and government deficits reached new levels. By 2009, however, the unprecedented amount of deficit spending stoked a new round of fear and anger. Emotions ran so high that the actions taken by democratically-elected leaders were labeled "tyranny" and the sense of outrage seemed destined to spark renewed efforts to reduce the deficits. In the years that have followed, some progress on deficit reduction was made, but widely-supported solutions evaded policy makers because so many players were responding only to an overly narrow range of emotions, refusing to make connections with the broader range of community feelings being fanned by the deficit problem.

The use of emotion does not always lead to good policy making. It is more likely to do so, however, when we cultivate a full range of emotions, when we come to understand the weight that should be given to many emotional responses. The best counterweight to feelings that distort our perception and judgment is an appreciation of additional emotional responses that broaden our understanding and enhance our judgment.

One technique for achieving this expanded understanding is to recognize the dearest emotional attachments of others, especially others with whom we disagree, and make some attempt to respect them, and integrate them into our analysis of policy. Thus, pro-life advocates would not cease to feel strongly about unborn children, but they would try to become more sensitive to the anguish of a pregnant rape victim, to the scarred lives unwanted children might lead, or to the harm that may come from illegal abortions. Similarly, pro-choice advocates would strive to understand the abortion issue from the point of view of those who sincerely believe that an abortion is murdering a human being, and the emotional reactions that inevitably flow from that starting point.

As we expand the reach of our affective connections, we will inevitably encounter competing emotions. In any important controversial policy debate, emotional considerations will emerge that pull us in different directions. How do we respond to such conflicting impulses? Saying that emotions should count does not end the story if different emotions count in favor of different policies. Indeed, one of the most difficult tasks in cultivating the use of emotions is to learn how to balance conflicting emotions and to not be overwhelmed by one particular emotion.

Weighing conflicting arguments that include affective dimensions is not fundamentally different than weighing purportedly unemotional conflicting arguments. Sometimes the conscious acknowledgement of feelings will simplify the deliberative process; sometimes it will complicate the process. But as a general proposition, a broader range of deliberation that relies on a broader range of human capacities will yield a more thorough airing of problems and more satisfactory solutions. Sometimes, witnessing human misery and the depth of suffering a policy has caused may lead to a re-evaluation of that policy. An appreciation of the emotional attachments that are important for another person will not always change one's policy position. But this valuing of the concerns of others creates a different kind of policy discourse than the one that results when people on each side immediately focus on their own feelings, and shut out those of others. And everyone in a position to make policy should attend to the emotional attachments of those whose voices are less likely to be heard, whose feelings are more likely to be ignored.

Both reason and emotion should play major roles in public policy decisions. Emotional appeal cannot be the sum total of policy analysis and argumentation. We can, however, recognize a legitimate, acceptable place for appropriate emotional responses in discussions of public policy. Appropriate responses are those that are relevant to the circumstances in which they arise, and to the cause for which they are being marshaled. We should tend to a wide range of emotional responses, being open to the full scope of affective concerns in a way that enhances full community dialogue, and deepens our understanding of what the five benchmarks mean as we address our societal problems.

A Preview

A brief consideration of one particular case provides a preview of how the five benchmarks can be used, before we proceed to a more in-depth presentation of each of them. In 2013, Edward Snowden leaked information about National Security Agency (NSA) surveillance programs. The resulting national discussion provided examples of how emotional responses enter into policy discussions, as the public discourse touched on such topics as spying on the American people, lying to Congress, massive evasions of the law, invasions of privacy, all under the specter of secret court decisions. On the other side of the debate the talk was of the duty to protect innocent lives as a war on terror was being waged against insidious foes, some of whom had infiltrated American society, who were fanatically determined to carry out new operations like the 9/11 attacks. Snowden was alternately hailed as a hero or condemned as a traitor.

The press presented the disclosures about the NSA programs as a classic case of balancing security and liberty, and it was that. But a journey through the five benchmarks of benefit, effectiveness, fairness, fidelity and legitimacy reveals a much more complicated picture.

In May, 2013, Snowden revealed information about several top-secret U.S. and U.K government mass surveillance programs to the British newspaper *The Guardian*. These programs included the interception of United States and European telephone activity, and the monitoring of Internet communications—activity which resulted in the tracking of cellphone calls and monitoring the e-mail and Internet traffic of nearly all Americans. Snowden fled the country and was eventually granted asylum in Russia. He was charged with three felony counts, including violations of the U.S. Espionage Act. Snowden justified these leaks as an attempt "to inform the public as to that which is done in their name and that which is done against them."

The primary rationale for the NSA surveillance programs is the *benefit* they provide. They reduce the number of terrorist attacks. The more our national security agencies know, the safer we are. NSA Director General Keith Alexander announced that the controversial intelligence-gathering programs had prevented 54 terrorist attacks around the world, including 13 in the United States. Critics of the programs were skeptical of that claim, and identified costs and risks on the other side of the benefit ledger, including violations of individual liberties, invasions of privacy, loss of trust in the government, and huge expenditures.

One question *effectiveness* asks is whether those attacks could have been prevented by other, less costly means. Were some of the costs inherent in these kinds of activities? Were other costs linked to how the programs were implemented? Could the same data have been collected in a more transparent way, if not more transparent to the general public, at least more transparent to the Congress or other oversight bodies—such as a court shrouded in less secrecy than the Foreign Intelligence Surveillance Court? A more transparent operation might have avoided to some extent the loss of trust in government that followed the revelation of excesses. However, suggestions of less secretive operations prompted many reactions similar to General Alexander's: "If we tell everyone exactly what we're doing, then the adversaries will know exactly how to get through our defenses." This assertion certainly has a ring of truth to it.

There is another question that effectiveness asks: if the same level of preventing terrorist attacks could *not* have been achieved without the secrecy, should we be willing to accept a lower level of success as a tradeoff for lowered costs? For example, would three more successful terrorist attacks over the 12 year period have been preferable if we could have avoided some of the invasions of privacy? Is prevention of all terrorist attacks, no matter what the cost, the only acceptable policy goal? How do we determine the level of risk that we should be willing to bear to maintain our current freedoms?

Fairness is about people receiving the treatment they deserve, getting what they are due, and in the case of the NSA surveillance programs, one fairness-based focus is on privacy. A general starting point is the belief that people are due a sphere of private activity that is beyond the reach of the government. The NSA programs exist, however, within a web of government surveillance policies that distinguish among different types of people, which in turn creates varying judgments about the privacy that is deserved for these different types.

One such distinction is between the gathering of intelligence on foreigners and on U.S. citizens. Foreign intelligence powers come from Presidential Executive Order 12333 and are overseen by the Executive Branch and Congress. Because of a sense that U.S. citizens deserve greater protection from their own government, an additional layer of oversight was established in the Foreign Intelligence Surveillance Court (FISC) by the Foreign Intelligence Surveillance Act to govern activities when U.S. citizens are involved. Even greater intrusions into individuals' privacy are permitted through the use of warrants when agents are dealing with known terrorists or suspected terrorists—individuals who by their own actions are deemed to have surrendered some of their privacy rights. Distinctions are also drawn between the types of privacy invasions, with the creation of a log of one's communications (the metadata) being seen as less of a violation of privacy than agents listening to phone calls or reading the contents of emails.

The fairness question addresses the treatment of groups of people and of individuals. When the focus is on privacy, do the NSA surveillance programs, as well as the broader web of policies, properly respect privacy rights? Are the differences in the treatment of different groups (U.S.

citizens, U.S. residents, "foreigners") fairly drawn among them? Are individuals who are singled out for more invasive surveillance fairly treated? And, at the policy level, are adequate safeguards created and maintained to assure that the number of instances in which persons receive less than they deserve are minimized? Were purported fairness standards breached when a program to create social network profiles of foreigners was expanded in 2010 to include American citizens?

Fidelity assesses the extent to which the surveillance programs complied with governmental commitments. The NSA programs appeared to encompass activities that were in accord with legal requirements, as they were approved by the Congress, the courts, and two administrations. Facts came to light, however, which called into question the congruence between the programs as approved and the programs in actual practice. For example, NSA collected 58,000 domestic communications a year, including data that were entirely domestic, for three years ending in 2011—actions that went beyond the agency's authority under Section 702 of the Patriot Act. What weight should this be given when judging the surveillance programs as a whole? (At least one Republican legislator raised the possibility of impeaching President Obama for improper use of the Patriot Act.) How much difference does it make that NSA discovered the problems (which it labeled mistakes rather than overreach), reported them to the court, and according to subsequent FISC opinions in 2012, had taken steps that resolved the matter? While legislative oversight is built into the design of the programs, many legislators said that NSA misled Congress. Are such failures in communication fatal flaws in the operation? Or do we presume that secret national security programs inevitably entail such things, and that we just don't want to know the truth?

The programs may also run afoul of external standards that are important to us when we evaluate U.S. government activities. Edward Snowden asserted that Article 12 of the Universal Declaration of Human Rights prohibits such systems of massive, pervasive surveillance. He also justified his own actions in terms of a principle he drew from the Nuremberg Trials: "Individuals have international duties which transcend the national obligations of obedience. Therefore individuals have the duty to violate domestic laws to prevent crimes against peace and humanity from occurring." Should an assessment of the fidelity of the NSA programs include a serious consideration of such external standards?

There is little doubt, if any, that a *legitimate* purpose of government is to prevent harm to its citizens through an effective national security program. Providing for the common defense is perhaps the least contested grounds for government programs. Yet even the legitimacy of the policies designed to protect the nation's security can be called into question. Is it legitimate for the government, especially in a democratic society, to pursue policies that are contrary to the will of the people?

Following Snowden's leaks about the NSA programs, some opinion polls showed that most Americans were supportive of these efforts to keep the nation safe. But opinion polling results are often quite fluid, particularly in cases in which new information comes to light over a period of time. After an extended period of Congressional hearings and new reports, a loss of public support for these programs could call into question the legitimacy of continuing those operations. The question is one of moral legitimacy rather than Constitutional legitimacy. Even when the President and Congress follow all legal standards for enacting policies, and those policies are carried out in perfect conformity to legal requirements, it is possible for the legitimacy of those actions to be called into question when they lack support among the general populace.

Notes

1 This distinction has been suggested in the analysis of legal argumentation by James Murray, "Understanding Law as Metaphor," *The Journal of Legal Education*, vol. 34 (1984), pp. 714–30.
2 Dividing approaches to ethics into a specific number of different options is an ever-evolving and fluid exercise. For example, Tom Beauchamp and James Childress, in their landmark *Principles of Biomedical Ethics* (New York: Oxford University Press, 7th ed., 2012, n. 1) expanded the types of ethical theories they described from two types (utilitarian and deontological) in their 1979 second edition to eight in their 1994 fourth edition, before narrowing the field to five in the 2001 fifth edition.
3 Mill wrote the definitive *Utilitarianism* in 1861. See Henry R. West, *An Introduction to Mill's Utilitarian Ethics* (Cambridge: Cambridge University Press, 2004) for a commentary on and interpretation of the classic text.
4 William K. Frankena, *Ethics*, 2nd ed. Englewood Cliffs, N.J.: Prentice-Hall, 1973, pp. 43–4.
5 Albert R. Jonsen and Stephen Toulmin, *The Abuse of Casuistry: A History of Moral Reasoning*. (Berkeley: University of California Press, 1988), p. 18.
6 H. Richard Niebuhr, *The Responsible Self: An Essay in Christian Moral Philosophy* (New York: Harper and Row, 1963), pp. 47–68.
7 Carol Gilligan, "Remapping the Moral Domain: New Images of Self in the Relationship," in Carol Gilligan, Janie Victoria Ward and Jill McLean Taylor (eds.) *Mapping the Moral Domain* (Cambridge, MA: Harvard University Press, 1988), pp. 3–19.
8 See Virginia Held, *The Ethics of Care: Personal, Political and Global* (New York: Oxford University Press, 2006).
9 This contrast is suggested by Rand Jack and Dana Crowley Jack in *Moral Vision and Professional Decisions: The Changing Values of Women and Men Lawyers* (Cambridge, MA: Harvard University Press, 1989).
10 John Rawls, *A Theory of Justice* (Cambridge, MA: Harvard University Press, 1974), p. 20.
11 When the time came in 2013 to decide if the United States should intervene militarily in Syria, Ross Douthat reviewed the list of benefits that had been offered for the Iraq War. Douthat concluded, at least in the Syrian case, that the only benefit that could truly be connected to the use of military force was maintaining U.S. credibility around the world to punish leaders who act badly, after the President had promised to do so. Ross Douthat, "War, What Is It Good For?" *The New York Times*, September 1, 2013, p. SR-11.

3   Defining the Good
Benefit

Perhaps the most widely-accepted assumption in the assessment of public policy is that we want policies to provide benefits to some or all members of a society. Indeed, for some observers, creating benefit is the sole goal in the making of policy.[1] Public policy *is* concerned with increasing the well-being of people and good policies are the ones that produce this result. Such understandings about policy evaluation are so common, in fact, that it is all too easy to agree that policies or policy proposals should be judged by the benefit they create without attending to some fundamental questions about the nature of the concept of benefit. The preamble of our Constitution expresses the intent to "secure the blessings of liberty to ourselves and our posterity." But what are those blessings? We should be asking such questions as: What is a benefit? Who decides whether a particular result is beneficial and on what grounds should they make that decision? How should we measure different, incommensurable benefits?

What Is a Benefit?

The beginning point for an ethical evaluation of the concept of benefit is to recognize the distinction between "effect" and "benefit." We can identify, project, measure or speculate about the effects that result from any public policy. Deciding whether those effects are beneficial or harmful is an altogether different matter—requiring an evaluation of results in light of moral notions of what is good or right. Effects that are worthy of the label "benefit" are those that improve our state of affairs by increasing the amount of things that are considered good (or decreasing the amount of things that are considered bad), and those judgments about what is good or bad rely on particular sets of values. The key to such assessments, of course, lies in which values are to be controlling in making these judgments.

Consider, for example, one bit of fallout from the Denver Income Maintenance Experiment in the 1970s.[2] This program was administered by the Department of Health, Education and Welfare in an effort to determine to what extent, if any, recipients of a guaranteed income would change their behavior (in particular, whether they would work less). Families participating in the experiment received income payments. They agreed to report any other income and household composition each month and to be interviewed several times a year.

One story from that experiment illustrates the point I want to make. One husband in the experimental group thought that he had been harmed by this program because his wife divorced him. He believed that the experiment had given her the financial independence she needed to leave him. The wife, no doubt, considered this outcome to be a benefit of the experiment.

The same kind of divide was evident in 2013 as Congress struggled to pass a comprehensive immigration bill. The choice between large-scale deportation of undocumented workers and the establishment of broad pathways to citizenship would certainly affect the size of the American labor force and in turn likely impact wage rates. Not surprisingly, differences of opinion about whether a smaller workforce would be desirable emerged between those who were paying wages and those who were receiving them. Similar differences of opinion exist about whether the effects of policies are beneficial which make same-sex marriage available to more couples, increase the number of assault weapons owned by American citizens, or eliminate penalties for the use of marijuana.

Benefit is a multi-faceted concept. One readily understood type of benefit is financial gain, as measured through economic analysis. We also recognize the plural nature of benefit: people also value such things as life, health, liberty, beauty, peace and knowledge. Since policies which aim to increase these many different things are deemed to be beneficial, our notion of benefit should not be reduced to a single type of value. Some efforts at measuring benefit have sought to assign a dollar value to everything people value, as a way of comparing benefits and costs that are fundamentally different in nature.

A danger of this approach is an oversimplification of what we as a society value. These monetizing techniques to establish dollar values on a single scale cannot easily answer questions about radically different kinds of results. For example: Is the loss of family farms as a consequence of the more efficient production of food by large agri-businesses a harm or a benefit? Governmental policy can encourage or discourage the development of closer ties between universities and private industries. Are such closer relations a benefit, because they create a more effective research establishment, or a harm, because they threaten the intellectual independence of the academy? Different answers are given by people who are situated differently, and it is highly questionable that assigning dollar values to these various results could resolve those differences.

Our understanding of what is a benefit can also be enhanced by keeping in mind the difference between intrinsic value and instrumental value. Some results of policies are considered benefits because they are intrinsically valued, because those consequences are considered to be good in and of themselves and are valued for their own sake. Other results may be deemed to be benefits because those results are, in turn, instrumental in the pursuit of other valued purposes. The significance of the difference between these two types of values can be illustrated by the difference between arguing that we should protect endangered species for their own sake and arguing for such protection because of the benefit that those species provide to humanity. Do we want to protect wilderness areas and pristine beaches for their intrinsic worth or for the benefit humans derive from them? A commitment to the intrinsic valuing of animals and nature supports a different kind of argument than does an instrumental approach to environmental policies. An instrumental view of protecting species readily allows for trading off the well-being of a species if benefits to humans are secured. Intrinsic valuation resists such easy tradeoffs.

While issues related to the environment and animal rights provide some of the most obvious distinctions between intrinsic and instrumental value, this is a distinction that can make a difference in other policy areas as well. Do we punish criminals for intrinsic reasons (what the individual deserves) or instrumental reasons (deterring other potential wrong doers)? The welfare debate has raised the question of whether there is something intrinsically valuable about working. Is laboring primarily of instrumental value, valued only as a way of acquiring goods and contributing to society, or is it an activity of intrinsic worth? The answer to this question can shape one's assessment of "workfare" or other programs that tie government benefits to the recipients' activities as workers.

Many "workfare" arguments seem to rely on a view of work as intrinsically valuable. According to this view, there is something good about working, in and of itself, and thus putting people to work can be calculated as a benefit of a policy. If, however, working is intrinsically valuable, what does that say about policies that allow individuals to avoid working by living off inherited wealth? On the other hand, if working is valued only instrumentally, if there is no inherent value in a person working simply to be working, then the argument for "workfare" may lose some of its force.

Whether a benefit is valued intrinsically or instrumentally depends on where the answers to the "why" question stop. Why is this end good? As a parent I discovered that if children kept asking "why?" long enough, my answer eventually came to, "Because I said so." The same is true in ethics, when an advocate reaches a point where she is at a loss to say *why* we should believe something. The question could be "Why should we value human well-being?" or "Why should we obey the will of God?" or "Why should we be moral?" Eventually the conversation arrives at bedrock starting points, which are matters of faith, and the best that one can say is something like: If you don't share my belief that this is valuable, then we really don't have much of a basis for continuing the discussion.

Clifford Geertz tells a story that illustrates this reality:

> There is an Indian story—at least I heard it as an Indian story—about an Englishman who, having been told that the world rested on a platform which rested on the back of an elephant which rested in turn on the back of a turtle, asked (perhaps he was an ethnographer; it is the way they behave), what did the turtle rest on? Another turtle. And that turtle? "Ah, Sahib, after that it is turtles all the way down."[3]

When you get to the turtles, you know you have ended the instrumental regress and arrived at intrinsic value.

Which Benefits? Pragmatic Concerns

Which consequences of a policy should be included in assessing the potential benefits or harms? The seemingly obvious answer is "all of them." In practice, however, there are reasons—some practical and some principled—for restricting the range of benefits and harms to be included in any analysis.

Benefits and harms can be conceived as running along a continuum, from a thin conception of benefit that focuses on physical well-being to thicker conceptions that include considerations that might be raised under such labels as psychological, spiritual, or aesthetic. Which harms are to be recognized in policy discussions? Some analyses rely on a thin conception of harm, focusing on the risks of deaths, disease or injuries, and often include financial considerations. A thick conception of harm incorporates a broader range of losses and damage, including such social harms as social disruption, the abandonment of certain conventions and values, and the undermining of political and social institutions.

The 1979 accident at Three Mile Island (TMI) illustrates the difference between these two conceptions of harm. When the nuclear power plant near Middletown, Pennsylvania, suffered a partial core meltdown, the radiation released from the plant was relatively small. Not a single person died in the accident and few, if any, cancer fatalities were expected to result from it. But for some observers, the negative societal impact was enormous. The accident devastated the utility that owned and operated the plant. It has been argued that the accident imposed enormous costs (estimated as high as $500 billion) on the nuclear industry and on society through stricter regulations, reduced operations of reactors, reliance on more expensive energy sources and increased costs of reactor construction and operation. The accident may have also led to more reliance on coal and oil as sources of energy, which may have in turn contributed to climate change. Is this the kind of harm that should be associated with such a mishap? Was much of that $500 billion spent in the aftermath of TMI spent beneficially to produce a safer environment through improved safety and equipment in other nuclear power plants? The answer to that question may depend on the "thickness" of one's view of "safe."

When we use the thicker concepts of benefit, the scope of the results that are considered expands. In practice, however, limits must be set on the range of consequences that enter into the assessment process. As a practical matter the range of consequences being reviewed cannot be limitless. Only finite amounts of time and resources can be, or should be, devoted to a single problem or issue. As the scope of potential benefits expands, at some point, we reach the limits of the usefulness of the tools and techniques that are available to us. Any feasible approach to assessing benefits must take into account the three issues of (1) foreseeability, (2) remote and diffuse consequences, and (3) multiple policy options.

The first difficulty is foretelling the future. The obvious limits we encounter are captured in the title of a 1999 article in *Business Week* magazine: "What Do You Call an Economist with a Prediction? Wrong." *The New York Times* updated this sentiment in 2010 by putting this headline on a column: "Often Wrong, But Never in Doubt." The task of evaluating results is enormously complicated by the fact that any evaluations that have any relevance to current policy debates are never simply a matter of reviewing the past. The results of existing policies continue in the present and into the future. Assessments of proposed policies are based exclusively on projections and probabilities. Thus, calculating benefit is not a matter of investigating past events but of predicting the likelihood of alternative futures. Predicting diverse and remote futures is risky business. Making policy in the real world is difficult because we cannot know with certainty the benefits or harms that will result from the implementation of any particular policy. Even as a deficit reduction agreement was being reached in August, 2011, respected economists were widely divided about whether the change would abet or abort the gradual recovery from the Great Recession.

We want to know the odds and to make optimal decisions based on our best calculations of future probabilities, sometimes forgetting that the worst result, even if statistically less likely, is still a possibility. The task of modeling alternative futures is especially daunting when the analyst is expected to place probability estimates on events that have never occurred. In these types of cases, we are thinking in terms of theoretical probabilities rather than frequencies. Some events—such as automobile accidents—occur so frequently that we can generate data that enable the production of reliable estimates. But unique events, or those that are at present only hypothetical realities, make risk calculation exceedingly speculative. At some points we must simply acknowledge that we are not dealing with reliable odds but with unknown futures.

The challenge of foreseeability is compounded by the complexity of modern society and scope of governmental activity. Contemporary problems are so dynamic and intertwined, and government programs and activities are so numerous and interdependent, that predicting results with any degree of accuracy is increasingly problematic. Any public policy sets into action an ever-expanding set of consequences, like the ripples caused by a rock that is tossed into a pond. One major task for any assessment of benefits and harms flowing from a policy is to determine how remote the consequences must be before they should not be factored into the analysis. Our ability to project with any certainty the consequences that will follow from an action diminish fairly rapidly as we move away from the site of the action in time and space. For example, to use two extreme hypotheticals related to the building of nuclear power plants: Should a decision to prohibit the construction of additional nuclear reactors factor in the possibility that a shortage of energy could develop that could exacerbate conflict in the Middle East, leading to a general war that would result in the destruction of the state of Israel? Or, on the other hand, should a decision to promote greater construction of reactors factor in the possibility that increased reliance on nuclear power could result in massive unemployment in the coal-producing state of West Virginia that could lead to civil unrest and disorder? The task we face is one of drawing lines. Limits will be set on how far we go in following speculative ripples to the edge of the pond, as we seek to evaluate possible benefits and harms.

Chaos theory explains in a fairly dramatic way the importance of this problem. The core of chaos theory is not that events happen without cause. Chaotic phenomena, rather, are understood to be a class of deterministic processes that *seem* to mimic random dynamics. Thus, one fundamental characteristic of them is a lack of predictability—not because causal relationships do not exist but because those relationships are beyond our ability to discover them. Chaos behavior has been described as order masquerading as randomness. Order takes on this appearance of randomness because it is impossible to monitor all of the elements, forces, and interactions that create our future. If, as we've been told, it is impossible to monitor dozens of species in a mountain range, and even dozens of fluctuating reaction products in a laboratory vessel,[4] then it is surely impossible to precisely monitor thousands and millions of human and natural interactions in a modern society.

If the lesson to be learned from chaos theory is that measurements can never be perfect, that lesson becomes more significant when it is magnified by what has been called the catastrophe effect: seemingly insignificant variations in conditions can result in dramatic differences in outcomes. An illustration from the physical world is the avalanche that is caused by the last snowflake to fall on a ledge or a minor change in temperature. Because of these tipping points, what appear to be minor changes in our social environment, or tiny inaccuracies in our measurements of the social world, can yield large, unanticipated consequences. No matter how exhaustive we are in our efforts to be precise, our projections will inevitably be suspect and they will become increasingly so as we move away from the initial site of policy action.

Since policy evaluation always entails comparisons of policy options, the difficulty of the task of projecting probabilities is multiplied by the number of alternatives under consideration. The need for comparative assessments highlights a second kind of line that must be drawn: how many options should we study? How many policy options must be explored before concluding that a particular alternative is the most beneficial choice possible?

At the core of the pragmatic limits to the range of benefits that we can take into account are the availability of time and resources to project results, and the reliability of the techniques available to make these projections. Some effects are too remote to calculate reasonably. Some are too remote to be significant. The American experience in the war in Iraq has demonstrated what every soldier knows: one thing we know about war is that things never go according to plan. All too often, this lesson applies to making public policy. Chaos theory supports the sense that our judgments about what is insignificant are of questionable certainty. It is this uncertainty which undermines the feasibility of some projections and establishes practical limits to the amount of resources that should be devoted to others.

Which Benefits? Principled Concerns

Whose Benefits?

Some benefits and harms are excluded from policy evaluations for principled reasons. As a society, we have chosen to exclude the benefits and harms that result for some persons, and to discount the value of benefits for others. An obvious example is the benefit obtained through criminal activity. An occasional economist has argued that the loss that criminals suffer as a result of law enforcement activity should be included as harms when we assess our policies which impose punishment for unlawful behavior. As a community, however, we have determined that certain gains are illicit and that a thief should not profit from his crimes. If a thief has broken the law and is subsequently required to surrender stolen property, we do not consider this to be harm suffered by that person when we assess that policy of punishment. We exclude these costs and harms from policy evaluations on principled grounds. (The concern for proportionality in punishment will be addressed later in the section on fairness.)

While a thief would view a reduction in his profit from criminal activity as a cost of an enforcement policy, as a society we do not view these reductions in this way. A community can make judgments that certain conduct is not legitimate. A criminal fine or incarceration is not a matter of setting a price for those who want to engage in certain activity—rather, it is punishment in an effort to prevent the activity altogether. If some benefits and harms are to be excluded in policy-making calculations, the issue can be framed in terms of "standing."[5] Whose preferences are to be counted? Or whose welfare should be considered? In both questions, the issue is who has standing in our deliberations. The next sections identify three specific examples of how these questions arise.

Animals and Nature

The extent to which the well-being of animals should be included in the measurement of the benefit and harm of public policies is a hotly-debated issue.[6] Regulations prohibiting cruelty to animals are common, reflecting some societal consensus that our treatment of non-human animals is an appropriate matter for government concern. Even this consensus provides an uncertain point of departure. Is the justification for such regulation based on the effect that the prohibited conduct has on humans—offending their particular cultural sensibilities, or desensitizing people to violence that might have consequences for the treatment of humans? This approach accords only an instrumental value to animals. Or is the regulation grounded in an intrinsic valuing of the well-being of animals (or certain animals)—which could provide a springboard for other regulations protecting animal rights?

Determining whether benefits and harms to animals fall within the scope of the effects to be considered in policy discussions is complicated by the variety of potentially affected activities (such as animal experimentation, environmental protection and development, hunting, breeding and rearing animals for food, care of domestic animals, religious sacrifice) and the range of beings within the animal kingdom (running, for example, from invertebrates to dolphins and chimpanzees). While reliable figures on the number of experiments performed on animals are difficult to confirm, there is no doubt that such experimentation is widespread (some sources estimate experimentation on 20 million animals in the United States each year). Many of these experiments inflict pain on animals; some result in the animal's death. Animals have been used to test the efficacy and toxicity of drugs, and the skin and eye irritancy of shampoo and cosmetics. Animals have been used in research on cancer, surgery and artificial insemination, and in weapons and safety testing. The justification for this experimentation is that the activity provides a benefit to humans, that our bodies are healthier and our environment is safer as a result of this experimentation. If such benefits were not secured, the expenditure of research funds would be difficult to justify. If such benefits to humans are secured, the remaining issue is whether, and to what extent, the harm done to animals should provide a basis for restricting or prohibiting certain types of experimentation.

Many observers argue that the pain suffered (and pleasure enjoyed) by animals should count in our assessment of the effects of our actions. They argue that animals are not simply expendable, available for exploitation for human ends, and that disregarding their suffering is a form of speciesism. This approach does not necessarily require a positing of "equal worth" among all species. The key ground for drawing distinctions for some commentators is suffering. The implication is that harm to animals enters into the calculation only in the case of animals that are sentient or that have the capability to experience suffering. Thus, experimentation on animals is justifiable only if pain is kept to a minimum and the research is likely to produce benefits that outweigh the animals' pain.

This type of balancing was evident in the Great Ape Protection Act being considered by the Senate in 2012. The act would have phased out, over a three-year period, invasive experimentation on chimpanzees—unless it became necessary to address a new, emerging or re-emerging disease. It would also permanently retire hundreds of chimps owned by the National Institutes of Health. That legislative session ended without the bill coming to the floor for a vote.

Cross-Border Effects

If a policy affects the residents of other countries, should the benefits and harms to these foreigners be treated in the same manner as those to residents of the country that is evaluating the policy? Do we get the same answer when we ask if a U.S. state's policy assessment should consider equally the effect on residents of a different state? Or if a city's policymakers should give equal consideration to effects on residents in a neighboring county?

One possible answer is that the appropriate reference group for counting benefits and harms includes all individuals affected by a policy regardless of nationality or place of residence. This view is especially persuasive in cases in which one group acts to achieve benefits for themselves, but harms are suffered by others across the border. Acid rain and downstream pollution provide examples of how the action of one city, state or nation can cause severe harm to another. These concerns support the conclusion that a full accounting of a policy's effects should include all affected parties.

The opposite conclusion is based on a view that policy evaluation should recognize the role borders play in assigning benefit and harm. The same effect can be a benefit in one jurisdiction and a harm in another, as is the case in times of war: is the death of an enemy soldier a benefit or a harm? The development of wartime policy depends on inflicting harm on those on the "other side," harms that are viewed as instrumental benefits by those developing the strategy for inflicting death. Even in the absence of armed conflict, the military competition between nations, such as we saw in the Cold War, can produce effects on friends and enemies that yield opposing judgments about benefit.

In the more benign world of economic competition, borders create varying assessments of benefit. The development or strengthening of a domestic industry is a benefit at home but a harm to the parallel industry in a competitor nation. The same holds true for decisions about tax subsidies to domestic agri-businesses and the effect of those policies on family farms in less developed countries. In the current debates over immigration, and the re-opening of the North American Free Trade Agreement, many participants object on principle to an evaluation of U.S. policies that take into account, on anything approaching an equal basis, the benefits to the citizens of Mexico. Within the same national boundaries some would find unreasonable a requirement that a state consider the harm done to the economy of another state when, for example, deciding whether to provide tax incentives to lure a corporation to move its headquarters, or to engage in a public relations campaign to attract more tourists. In 2008, the state of Georgia raised a claim that its boundary with Tennessee should be redrawn to correct a surveying mistake made two centuries earlier, a correction that would solve serious water problems by giving Georgia access to the Tennessee River. Few, if any, Tennessee legislators gave any weight to the benefits that would flow to Georgia citizens from such a change as they announced their positions opposing the change. When Tennessee's Governor showed no interest in considering Georgia's position in 2013, Georgia's lawmakers threatened to take the case to the U.S. Supreme Court to force a result that would create a benefit on one side of that state boundary, perhaps at a cost to those on the other side.

Similar principled objections are routinely expressed to supporting policies being adopted in one jurisdiction because they would provide benefits elsewhere: Why should one group of taxpayers be expected to pay for a policy whose benefits are primarily secured for those outside the taxed population's boundaries? One answer to that question is: because those taxpayers want to provide those benefits. As we'll see in the section on preference-based utilitarianism, one way of identifying benefits to be served by public policy is to measure the preferences of individuals. So, for example, if U.S. taxpayers value the benefits that would accrue to foreigners through foreign aid policies or climate-change policies, then those benefits could be included. The crucial point to this approach is that the benefit is based on satisfying those domestic preferences, not in serving the welfare of foreigners; the benefits to foreigners are not valued in the same way that they would if those benefits were provided to U.S. citizens.

One alternative in the cross-border effects discussion is to count the benefits and harms of foreigners, but to count them as less than those of citizens. This results in separate calculations for the effects of a policy on the two different groups. But practical issues arise immediately in determining what percentage of the full benefits should be used for those who have less than full standing. We sometimes do include considerations of the effects of our policies on those who live beyond our borders, but usually in a way that is subordinate to the gains and losses or our own citizens.

Future Generations

Many public figures express concern for the well-being of future generations. When debating budget deficits or climate change or health care systems, the effect of present-day policies on future generations receives a lot of lip service. The extent to which a benefit to those not yet born actually affects current policy assessments, however, is limited by a mixture of principled and practical considerations.

A leading approach to identifying and measuring benefit relies on expressions of individual preferences, often in terms of what people are willing to pay for particular policy outcomes. If benefit is determined by the preferences that individuals express, future generations are excluded as a matter of principle. The members of those generations cannot express their wishes in the present; they simply are not here to reveal their preferences. As a practical matter, there is no way that they can make choices in the market now that reflect what they will someday deem to be beneficial. Those future generations are not here to vote, to advocate their causes, to form organizations and donate to political campaigns. It is possible to try to serve their welfare through some kind of substituted judgment by members of the present generation who care about the well-being of future cohorts. But studies consistently show that we routinely discount the benefit that policies provide to those not yet born—perhaps excessively so. Survey after survey has shown that the needs and desires of those of us now alive and making decisions are much more heavily weighted than those we project for generations to come.

This recognition of the devaluing of the interests of future generations raises similar questions about other groups in a community. This devaluing of interests can apply to members of our society who lack the visibility or the voice or the clout to have full standing in the process of identifying and measuring the beneficial consequences of policy decisions. We may be forced into a substituted judgment model for those who cannot register their own preferences, such as children and the mentally incompetent.

Other constituencies may find themselves disadvantaged in the typical calculations of benefit. For example, should we be concerned if mathematical models of calculating benefits and harms consistently place undesirable and hazardous sitings in the neighborhoods of certain minorities because property values are consistently lower there? Should we give more weight to the preferences or welfare of those most directly affected by a proposed toxic waste dump? Should we pay extra attention to the needs or welfare of those least able to defend or promote their own interests? Answers to such questions mingle concerns about benefit with those about justice and fairness, which will be addressed later.

Existence Value

"Existence Value" is a concept that provokes disagreement in discussions about which results should count as benefits. Existence value refers to the benefit people receive from the mere existence of a good, the value a person places on a particular state of affairs not because of any use or even direct experience with that reality but simply because she knows that that state of affairs exists. The essence of existence value is captured in the observation that there are many persons who obtain satisfaction from mere knowledge that part of the North American wilderness still exists, even though they would be appalled by the prospect of being exposed to it. Other terms that are used to refer to this type of value are non-use value (the benefit from a good that a person does not use), or option value (the benefit a person gains from having the option to use that good).

Some analysts think that existence value should be excluded from calculations of benefit. Many of the concerns about including considerations of existence value in policy analysis seem to be pragmatic rather than principled: the range of potential existence values is limitless, there is no practical way to identify all existence values, and it is impossible to measure accurately such values. While these concerns are practical in nature, they are so massive that they lead to questioning whether this whole category of benefits should, as a matter of principle, be excluded from the analysis of public policies.

It is important to emphasize that benefits related to existence value are not necessarily associated directly with the existing state of affairs but rather with the positive value that that state of affairs has for those who know about it—especially those who do not benefit in any direct way from that reality. Thus, the existence of a rare bird in the Amazon jungle yields existence value only if there are people who know of its existence and who value it. Critics are correct in noting that the world of existence value knows no bounds. All things that are valued (tall sand dunes at the beach, quiet streets, successful space missions, appropriate children's television programming, family farms, national energy self-sufficiency, winning Olympic medals, county fairs), even by people who have only remote knowledge of them, possess existence value.

One illustration comes from the cost-benefit assessments of building a dam on the Tuolumne River in California to produce hydroelectric power. The early estimates were positive: the value of the electricity that would be generated greatly exceeded the cost of construction. An alternative assessment was then developed that included the "option value" of the whitewater rafting on the river that would be lost if the dam were built—that is the amount *nonusers* would be willing to pay to preserve this recreational opportunity. The survey conducted to measure this value yielded an option value estimate of $33.5 million in additional costs, changing the outcome of the cost-benefit comparison from favorable to unfavorable.[7] Should the evaluation of all such intangible factors be allowed to reverse the outcome of comparing more direct costs and benefits? After all, determining the benefit of maintaining or enhancing all valued states of affairs is surely a quixotic quest. Anything that is valued by anyone, anywhere, counts.

On the other hand, these nonuse and nonconsumptive values are real. The well-being of people is enhanced or diminished as they think that these states of affairs are enhanced or diminished. Any assessment of a policy's benefit and harm that did not include these values would be incomplete. The fact that the measurement of these values eludes certain benefit measurement techniques may say more about the limitation of those approaches to determining benefit than it does about the proper scope of the harms and benefits that should be a part of policy analysis.

Public Preferences: Preference–Based Utilitarianism

As mentioned earlier, one approach to identifying benefit relies on public expressions of individual preferences. This approach is based on the belief that the individuals who are or will be affected by a policy are usually the best judges, or perhaps the only judges, of what is in their own interests. An extension of this view is that social welfare consists basically of an aggregation of individual well-being, an understanding that the public interest can be reduced to an accumulation of individual private interests.

This approach can be grounded in either utilitarian or libertarian philosophies. The utilitarian standard for judging policy is the production of the greatest good for the greatest number of people. For many utilitarians, the goal is to create the greatest balance of pleasure over pain, or the greatest net increase in happiness. Even for those utilitarians who describe the good in terms other than pleasure or happiness, the aim of public policy is to improve the lot of citizens by increasing the balance of things that are valued positively compared to things that are valued negatively. If the purpose of public policy is to make peoples' lives better, it is argued, the people best situated to determine whether a particular effect makes their lives better are those whose lives are being affected.

A libertarian may come to a similar conclusion about reliance on individual judgments as the best way to assess benefit and harm, but through a different argument. For the libertarian the starting point is autonomy, not utility. Respect for individual dignity requires that each person exercise as much self-determination as is consistent with the autonomy of other persons. To the extent that some collective action, such as governmental regulation, is necessary, respect for the dignity of individuals requires that such intrusions into personal lives be consistent with the individuals' values and preferences. The libertarian approach is oriented more toward process than substance. The conviction is not necessarily that individuals are, in fact, the best determiners of benefit. Rather, their autonomy requires that they be allowed to make those determinations, even if they get the answer "wrong" from some objective point of view. In either case, that policy is best which reflects what each person holds to be beneficial, allowing individuals to achieve what they deem to be good rather than imposing external values upon them.

Willingness to Pay (WTP)

There are different ways to identify and measure individual preferences. One method for accounting for benefit is based on the premise that each person's welfare is to count according to his or her own valuation. The challenge is to determine what those valuations are, especially in large aggregations of individual preferences. Cost-benefit analysis is a technique that is widely used to measure and compare benefits, as well as costs and harms. (In the chapter on Effectiveness, the balancing of benefits and costs will be taken up in more detail.) This measurement and comparison in cost-benefit analysis is accomplished by reducing the value of all of the effects of policies to a single standard of measurement—which is dollars. The monetizing of effects provides a feasible way to handle the otherwise wildly incommensurable results that flow from various policies. If it is difficult to compare apples and oranges (which policy is better, one that produces nine apples or seven oranges?), the level of difficulty soars when comparing megawatts of electricity and fly fishing. Assigning dollar value to all results is one way to address this difficulty.

Economists have devised multiple methods for assessing individuals' preferences, depending on the kind of benefits being considered. One of these methods is the empirical study of actual market transactions. In this model, the valuing of individuals is measured by their willingness to pay for certain results. As rational maximizers of self-interest, individuals reveal their preferences by the choices they make. The value of benefits is understood to be the sum of the maximum amounts that people are willing to pay to gain those outcomes that they view as desirable (or the amounts that they are willing to pay to avoid outcomes they view as undesirable). Thus, observing what people pay in a free market tells us what specific goods and services are worth. In some cases, monetary valuation is fairly straightforward: $100 in food stamps is worth $100. Housing with a rental value of $500 a month on the open market is worth $500.

However, market transactions do not exist for many of the goods and services that are considered to be beneficial consequences of a public policy. For these types of benefits, economists have developed the technique of shadow pricing, which uses evidence from market choices to create implicit markets for goods that are not themselves traded. The assumption is that people indirectly reveal their preferences for some benefits by the choices they make in purchasing other benefits. For example, models have been developed that use intercity salary differences to estimate the benefits of air quality improvements, and that use housing prices to estimate the valuing of health risks and the quality of public schools.[8]

Establishing the value for a statistical human life presents a unique challenge. While it is not usually debated whether preserving a human life is a benefit or not, the value of that benefit is exceptionally difficult to measure. Wage and price models assign value to human life by taking into account such factors as voluntary expenditures for safety devices, willingness to pay for life insurance, and the wage differentials actually required to induce individuals to accept hazardous employment. The conclusions reached in such exercises vary significantly. One study in 2007 calculated the implied value of one human life as varying between $98,463 and $6,031,019, based on purchases of safety devices and the risks that those devices reduced. For decades, executive orders issued by presidents have required economic impact analyses of all significant federal regulations. While more consistency among government analyses has developed over the past 20 years, in 2003 Kip Viscusi and Joseph Aldy still reported findings on the value of a statistical human life that ranged from $3 million in the Federal Aviation Administration to $6.3 million in the Environmental Protection Agency.[9] Their review of a variety of studies, governmental and non-governmental, led them to conclude that the value of a statistical life for prime-aged workers had a median value of about $7 million in the United States.

Elizabeth Anderson has raised doubts about the preferences that are revealed in studies that analyze behavior in the workplace in an attempt to calculate the value of life. She believes the statistics resulting from such studies are valid only if several assumptions are true: (1) that workers are free to choose, without duress, among a significant range of worthwhile alternatives; (2) that workers' choices reflect deliberation upon full information about the risks they encounter; (3) that workers' choices express their own valuations, not the valuation others make of their lives; (4) that workers choose only for their own welfare, and choices are not motivated by any sense of moral obligation or personal responsibility for the welfare of others; and (5) that workers care only about the relative tradeoffs of money and risk in evaluating the acceptability of risks.[10] Anderson believes that there are grounds for questioning each of these assumptions, and thus she doubts the validity of shadow pricing outcomes.

Contingent evaluation is a third way of identifying and measuring benefit, when real-life market transactions and shadow pricing are not reliable options. This approach is a survey-based method which uses questionnaires or interviews with individuals to estimate the dollar value of intangible or nonmarket goods. For example, following the *Exxon Valdez* disaster in Prince William Sound, the State of Alaska commissioned a study in which more than 1,000 subjects were asked how much they would be willing to pay to avoid a similar accident in the next decade. These subjects were not people living on the shores of Prince William Sound; they were Americans most of whom had never visited and would never visit the Sound. The typical response was approximately $30. From this data, the state inferred that Americans collectively would be willing to pay about $2.8 billion to avoid such an incident.[11] In the aftermath of such accidents, punitive damages are awarded by courts in addition to actual damages, as a way to punish defendants and thereby to deter blameworthy conduct in the future. In 2008, the U.S. Supreme Court reduced the punitive damages that had been imposed against Exxon/Mobil from $2.5 billion to $507 million. By that time, the company had already spent $2.1 billion in cleanup costs, paid $125 million in federal criminal fines and restitution, $900 million in natural resource restoration costs, and $303 million in voluntary settlements with private parties.

Survey techniques that assess contingent value are questionable for a number of reasons. Their conclusions are based on what people say they would do, not what they have done. Thus, surveys lack the real world grounding of actual market transactions, or even shadow pricing. The public tends to be overly generous with hypothetical payments, particularly if the posing of the questions does not remind them of the large number of possible hypothetical goods or the realities of limited income. One study showed that saving the whooping crane from extinction was valued at as much as $715 billion. Answers to survey questions are very sensitive to the wording of the questions. There can be problems in clearly communicating to respondents the good that is being valued, and slight changes in wording can produce significant differences in what purport to be measurements of the same goods. When concerns are raised about how the studies are conducted, the topic is often about technique or method, with an eye toward improving the ways in which individual preferences are revealed in the analysis of WTP. A different set of issues arises in discussions about the usefulness of the concept of willingness-to-pay itself.

Limits to Willingness to Pay

There are limits to the utility of the willingness-to-pay approach to identifying and valuing benefits. WTP is an attempt to mimic the marketplace and, as such, it is subject to limitations that parallel market failures. It is an article of faith among economists that markets direct resources to more highly valued uses—at least in the absence of market failure. But what goes under the rubric of "market failure" may describe substantial features of everyday life in the real world. Several types of circumstances called market failures challenge the basic assumption of an ideal competitive economy, and these failures can provide rationales for government interference with private behavior.

The basic market model aims to produce the most efficient allocation of goods and resources, with the ideal goal being a Pareto-efficient distribution of goods. Named after the Italian economist Vilfredo Pareto, Pareto efficiency refers to a distribution of goods in such a way that no one could be better-off without making someone else worse-off. The theory is that each person aims to make the best use of his or her resources, and that the cumulative result of all individuals making such choices will maximize the benefits that people want. However, economic reality does not correspond to this ideal model. Policy makers are often in the business of finding effective solutions to social problems in response to failures in the private market. While many believe that free choice, unfettered by government regulations and requirements, is ideally the best mechanism for achieving efficient outcomes in a society, market failures are a fact of life in the world we actually inhabit.[12]

Market failures that prevent an effective ordering of our communal existence include the imperfect competition that results from asymmetries of power amassed by monopolies and cartels. Transaction costs and informational deficits can interfere with efficient decision making, and public goods (such as clean air and national defense) by their nature do not lend themselves to efficient market exchanges. Market prices fail to incorporate the full costs to society when those costs are imposed on third parties—such as in the overexploitation of natural resources and pollution of the environment. The traditional solution has been to use the tax system to impose these social costs on the actor, thus using the government to re-align costs and benefits to improve efficiency. An illustration would be the imposition of a tax on carbon-based products to account for the contribution of these products to the climate change that negatively affects others.

"The Tragedy of the Commons" is a story that has been told in various versions about how individual economically rational choices in an unregulated market can produce undesirable consequences. Imagine a village with a common green on which each villager can graze his cattle. It is in each herder's interest to put each cow he acquires onto the land, even if the quality of the commons is damaged as a result of overgrazing. The herder receives all of the benefits from an additional cow, while the damage to the common is shared by the entire group. If all herders make this individually rational decision, this market failure would result in the depletion or even destruction of the commons, to the detriment of all.

Two fundamental reservations about using WTP and other market-based approaches bear noting: (1) If even the proponents of these techniques acknowledge that they are not appropriate in instances of market failure, and market failures are in evidence to some degree throughout our economic system, then the utility of these techniques is obviously limited. (2) Even when market failure is not demonstrable in a particular setting, some observers are uncomfortable with accepting market behavior and consumerist interpretations as normative for making public policy, especially in cases involving such matters as human life and health, and environmental quality.

Citizens, even in their roles as consumers, encounter information barriers, barriers which mean they cannot be expected to accurately assess the value of what is being delivered or promised—or at least they could not make these assessments at reasonable costs to themselves in time, energy and resources. So, even when individuals' preferences are ascertainable, these preferences might not coincide with what those individuals would prefer if they were more fully informed. What one prefers, or is capable of preferring, is also a function of numerous social forces and rests significantly on a sense of what futures a person believes are possible. Many potential preferences fail to become expressed preferences because individuals simply fail to think that achievement of that preference would ever be possible. These complications point to the illusory character of the notion that the public policy decision making process can be simply a matter of following existing individual preferences.

Non-Market Approaches to Public Preferences

Mark Sagoff has written about the difference between approaching public issues as matters for economic decisions or as matters for political decisions. The first approach evaluates policies in terms of efficiency or wealth-maximization, because the question is how much we are willing to pay for alternative realities. For Sagoff the problem with this approach is that it treats us only as consumers, and sometimes we also regard ourselves as citizens. We act as consumers to get what we want *for ourselves*. We act as citizens to achieve what we think is best *for the community*. We are able to choose goals for our community that are different from those we might pursue privately.[13] As citizens we can, and should, make societal decisions based on historical, religious, cultural, aesthetic or moral grounds that are not necessarily consistent with the motives that drive decisions in the market place. The political arena offers an alternative to the economic arena, with different ways of evaluating personal preferences, especially in a democracy. This model is one in which all citizens are entitled to participate on equal terms. Ideally, the coin of the realm is principled, reasoned arguments advanced in public deliberation. It is the strength of one's reasons, the coherence of one's position that counts, rather than how much one is willing to pay. Citizens and officials are called to evaluate reasons, rather than react uncritically to unexamined desires expressed by the willingness of others to pay for certain outcomes.

In this context, such techniques as cost-benefit analysis (CBA) appear to be anti-democratic. In its extreme form, CBA can be viewed as a radical paternalism in which efficiency and wealth maximization are imposed through economic calculations despite the judgments expressed by the populace through the political process. Of course, the reality of political discourse and decision making is far from the ideal sketched above. Some participants in the political process have greater power than others for reasons quite apart from the validity of their ideas. Disproportionate influence is often based on wealth. Citizens' access to information can be a factor. An unflattering assessment of the public's handling of a process for making a decision about the siting of a hazardous waste facility led two commentators to conclude: "It may be impossible to conduct a coherent public deliberation about risk with a population that is both under- and mis-educated about uncertainty and neurotically preoccupied with certain hazards to physical health."[14] These are the kinds of problems with public political discourse that cost-benefit analysis and other economic methods were designed to resolve—although a CBA based on revealed preferences would similarly be skewed by public misperceptions.

Whether they are ascertained by a willingness to pay or non-economic methods, a reliance on public preferences in determining which results are beneficial is akin to building a castle on shifting sands. Expressed individual preferences do not provide a firm grounding for policy making. Consider the issue of closing the U.S. prison at Guantanamo Bay, Cuba. By the fall of

2008, George W. Bush, the outgoing President, had concluded that the prison should be closed. During that time, Barack Obama was campaigning with a pledge that he would close that prison if elected. All public opinion polls showed substantial support among the public for the change. Yet, in May 2009, Congress overwhelmingly rejected funding to close the prison, with opinion polls just a few months later showing the public to be opposed to the closing by a two-to-one margin.

This story illustrates that preferences are endogenous, meaning that they cannot be taken as given (as exogenous) but rather they are formed and changed as individuals receive new information and hear new arguments. As individuals respond to their ongoing experiences and observations, their preferences are altered. In this case, the landscape was changed when the focus of the debate shifted from a general concern about what was in the security interests of the United States to a different question: Do you want the Gitmo detainees brought to the prisons in your home state?

If policy making were a matter of implementing the "will of the people," then in January of 2009, the congressional Republicans would not have resisted closing the prison. And in May of 2009, President Obama would have acquiesced in the public's judgment. But policy is not made this way; nor should it be. The premise of this book is that preferences can be changed, and should be changed, in response to powerful, convincing arguments. Persuasion is possible, by presenting new information, highlighting interests, or re-interpreting existing information and interests. Governors and citizens alike have a responsibility to continually engage in this deliberative process.

Even when it is working close to optimal potential, the political model requires someone to determine which are the most coherent arguments, which are the most appropriate arguments. If there is not some kind of assessment of the validity of public arguments, we end up with an aggregation of political voices that parallels the aggregation of economic voices. Thus, there is an important role for enlightened observers to play in our collective assessment of benefits, a role that can temper an unexamined reliance on expressed preferences—whether those preferences are expressed through markets or the political process.

Experts: Welfare-Based Utilitarianism

What if public preferences are wrong? Can there be a difference between the public's preferences and what those preferences ought to be? Surely some personal preferences are poorly informed, ad hoc, or based on whims. Because a utilitarianism that relies solely on expressed preferences to define the good offers no way to distinguish between enlightened preferences and delusional preferences, it is important to look at another type of utilitarianism, a welfare-based utilitarianism. In this alternative approach, good policies are not necessarily those that conform to the community's preferences but rather are those that promote the community's welfare.

A basic question about benefit is whether benefit should be determined by what people want, or by judgments made independently of personal preferences. Some people want to smoke, but it is difficult to call smoking beneficial when there is solid evidence that it is a self-destructive behavior. Even if measurements of individual preferences provide useful information about the allocation of resources to highly-valued uses, that determination may not be the only factor that a policy maker wants to consider. There may be times that decisions should be driven by benefits other than those identified by the preferences of individuals.

Paul Portney has developed a hypothetical problem that illustrates the dilemmas faced when popular opinion and the opinions of experts diverge on the issue of benefit.[15] He describes a community of 1,000 adults, which he calls Happyville, in which the drinking water supply is contaminated by a naturally occurring substance. Every resident believes that this substance is responsible for Happyville's above-average cancer rate and they insist that a treatment system be installed to remove the contaminant. Every resident is willing to pay $1,000 each year for the removal of the contaminant.

The top ten risk assessors in the world have tested the contaminant and found it to test negative for carcinogenicity, even at much higher doses than those to which the residents are exposed. While the experts acknowledge that no one could ever prove the substance to be harmless, all of the assessors would stake their professional reputations on it being so. Because of a deep-seated skepticism of government officials, the citizens of Happyville remain unconvinced and truly frightened, and are still willing to pay $1,000 per person per year for water purification. If one were to do a cost-benefit analysis on the installation of the water treatment system, what would the benefit side look like? Is it the $1 million the citizens are willing to pay? What about the experts' view that the system would provide no actual benefit at all in terms of safer drinking water?

Portney adds one other wrinkle to his hypothetical. He suggests that the reader also suppose an alternative scenario in which the contaminant is not naturally occurring but rather is the result of industrial contamination, that the $1,000 per person figure had been validated in a state-of-the-art contingent evaluation study, and that a lawsuit had been brought against the plant producing the substance. Would you then be willing, he asked, to support a judgment for damages against the company, again assuming that the world's best risk assessors found no evidence of carcinogenicity? Such scenarios are not completely fanciful. For example, the citizenry of Braintree, Massachusetts blocked the expansion of an existing hazardous waste transfer station even though the impact statement, accepted by the state, demonstrated that the project would actually *decrease* the risk of harm to the community by reducing outbound waste shipments and associated transportation risks.

There is no doubt that members of the public sometimes misunderstand the beneficial or harmful nature of actual or proposed policies. Neighbors have opposed the placing of a hospice for AIDS patients in their neighborhood because of a belief that AIDS is highly contagious. In the absence of any empirical evidence, another group of neighbors opposed the extension of a mausoleum out of a fear that it would contaminate their water supply. Sometimes partisans misuse statistics or other evidence. There is a good case to be made for relying on experts' knowledge rather than the often misguided public intuition, especially in highly technical areas such as managing environmental risks. The result of following experts' judgments, almost certainly, would be a reduction in illness, more lives saved, and a cleaner environment.

A similar reliance on scientific expertise is developing in health care policy where benefit is often measured quantitatively in something like quality-adjusted life years, instead of expressed preferences. The outcome measure that is increasingly utilized for assessing policy is the number of life years gained, adjusted by factors related to the quality of those years, as determined by medical experts. Experts point out that the willingness-to-pay approach to valuation gives more weight to the stronger preferences of sick persons, than to the weaker preferences of the healthy. The application of expressed individual preferences to matters of health policy often results in the allocation of resources to efforts at cure rather than in more effective efforts at prevention, and thus leads to suboptimal investment from the point of view of saving or extending human lives. Patient preferences play a role in showing support for longer, healthier lives, but the policy means for achieving that goal can be more soundly based on good data. A new label being used in the medical profession is "evidence-based medicine," which does lead one to ask what medicine had been previously based on.

The role experts play in the public policy making process is extensive. Experts provide the data that are often the means by which we determine whether there is a problem that needs to be addressed by public policy. Policy experts work to develop and implement theoretically optimal programs, to evaluate how the programs actually work and to determine whether they are accomplishing what was intended; and if they are not succeeding, to decide how they can be improved or discontinued. We rely on experts because the world is so complex. This reliance fades, however, when we encounter experts who don't agree. Experts' personal and professional values and beliefs influence their role in setting standards for public policy even when they appear to be dealing with purely factual questions. The environmental risks that have provoked the greatest public reactions are those for which there is considerable disagreement among experts. In the area of food and drug regulation, it seems that newspaper readers can now expect to regularly find a scientific conclusion about risk or safety that contradicts the accepted scientific wisdom of just a few years earlier. While it may appear that these scientific questions are matters for empirical determination, experts' opinions can be inconsistent, as a result of poor data, unreliable instruments, or a focus on a particular subset of causes.

There are also differences between what experts attempt to measure and what is important to the lay public. There is a difference, for example, between the risk of a harm and the anxiety associated with that risk. What citizens fear may not be so much a potential toxic spill as much as the anxiety they would suffer worrying about the possibilities of a spill. Even if experts are right that we have nothing to worry about from electromagnetic fields, home owners could still suffer real losses if potential real estate buyers are not convinced by the experts. And a compelling conclusion about the low probability of a serious risk materializing is not determinative for those who are less risk averse than the experts think they should be.

Despite these shortcomings, a welfare-based approach to utilitarianism, that relies on expert judgment rather than individual preferences, makes an important contribution to the policy making process. Cass Sunstein describes the cost that has accompanied the move in recent decades from welfare-based utilitarianism to a preference-based utilitarianism: "A system that takes existing private preferences as the basis for political choice will sacrifice important opportunities for social improvement on welfare criteria. This point is a crucial one in the early stages of utilitarian thought; it has been lost more recently with the shift from older forms of welfarism to the idea of 'revealed preferences'."[16] Long ago, our society rejected a form of governance akin to Plato's philosopher king. Public policy should be responsive to public desires and interests. However, some preferences have emerged from unjust backgrounds. Some are based on false information. Other preferences lead to human deprivation and misery. If we rely only on revealed preferences, to the exclusion of expert guidance, we will lose opportunities to secure important societal benefits—benefits that would be endorsed even by those whose expressed preferences would lead us in a different direction.

A Dynamic Interaction

The significance of the distinction between expert judgment and revealed lay preferences can be diminished in policy making assessments by increasing discourse between the two. Consider three alternative approaches in assigning the value of benefit and harm to particular outcomes: (1) accepting the preference of affected parties, (2) accepting the judgment of acknowledged experts, or (3) expecting the policymaker to receive input from each source and to make a reasoned decision. It is not helpful to think of citizens and experts as two separate groups, independently arriving at conclusions that are then fed into the policy making process. A better representation of the process is a more dynamic one which incorporates the continuing give-and-take between experts and lay persons. The preferences of citizens are not fixed and can be shaped by what experts tell them. This more dynamic collaborative model highlights the interplay between preferences and specialized knowledge. Values, perspectives, and definitions of interests change. This approach to understanding benefit does not simply accept individual preferences as fixed and unchanging but recognizes a role for education and persuasion. The results of studies, the conclusions of experiments, the projections of models, and other presentations of the findings of experts are fed into the public domain and these should form and shape common perceptions of benefit and harm. Similarly, the values, concerns and aspirations of a citizenry have an impact on the work of experts: influencing the questions that are asked, the way studies are conducted, the topics that are selected for examination—in addition to providing the societal baseline for determining what kinds of results are good or bad.

The gulf between the lay public and experts could be decreased if the public were forced to face tradeoffs that must be made. Not surprisingly, many times groups of people would prefer to ignore looming threats rather than to make sacrifices for the benefit of others. The public does possess the option of simply refusing to come to grips with problems that do not have pleasant solutions—even though the unpleasant solutions would be preferable to leaving the problem unresolved. The location of high-level radioactive waste facilities is one example of such a problem. Residents typically frame the choice as "here" versus "not here," and not surprisingly they choose "not here" and prevent the creation of such a facility. The cumulative result of all groups of residents making this choice is, of course, that no waste facility is built, an outcome that is increasingly dangerous to the nation as a whole. We can only hope that such stalemates can be overcome by the presentation of evidence from experts that convinces a group of residents that such a facility must be built (continued deferral is not an acceptable option), that the facility in their vicinity is indeed the safest disposal option available, and that continued opposition places more people at risk—including people whose communities are less suitable hosts for the facility than their own. Similarly, the financial threats to Social Security and Medicare have gone unaddressed because the general public refuses to endorse the required accommodations. The prospect of finding solutions to waste facilities and entitlement programs is decreased when demagogic politicians stoke an anti-intellectualism that is too prevalent in segments of our society.

The alternative is not, of course, to ignore the citizenry's expressed preferences and rely solely on the judgment of experts and specialists to determine what is beneficial. Any technical analysis includes subjective judgments. We know that the perceptions of such specialists in the public policy process can be shaped and skewed by their own positions. As for efforts to quantify benefit, the assignment of dollar value to benefits will at times be based on a certain amount of guesswork and often on tacit, unarticulated value judgments. The best we can do is to accept evidence from a variety of sources in our efforts to make judgments about what is beneficial—in full awareness of the partial value of every source.

Benefit-Based Policy Making

The purpose of this chapter is to describe the concept of benefit, to consider ways that we can determine whether particular effects are beneficial or harmful, and to measure the degree of harm and benefit produced. The focus here is on benefit, on the way we want policies to produce benefit, and on the pragmatic limits to the connections we can draw between present policies and the possibilities of future benefit. At this point, we can identify some key variables in achieving beneficial results in the face of an uncertain future.

It is important to operate with an expansive view of benefit, to not shrink our vision to what can be measured in dollars and cents. Monetization can be a useful tool in a narrow-range analysis in a specific case. There is a danger, however, that an over-reliance on economic models can lead to a transformation of societal values and priorities. In fact, we have already witnessed some instances of this transformation, where the measure of virtue is not what one does to serve others, enhancing their well-being, but rather how much one serves himself, enhancing his own fiscal balance sheet. Observing that the logic of the marketplace increasingly governs more of our lives, Michael Sandel cautions against the "expansion of markets, and of what markets value, into spheres of life where they don't belong."[17]

It is also important to ask how we should respond to unknown futures in our policy making. Our assumptions about the proper role of government will influence our responses. One response would be to decide that absent a reliable projection of a benefit there is no basis to support any policy initiative. For example, the way one responds to the discovery of a substance of unknown qualities in our environment can vary depending on how "big" a government is desired. A more restrictive view of legitimate governance might lead to the conclusion that no government resources should be expended until a clear harm has been identified. If an industrial plant is the source of the substance, no government interference is warranted until such a clear showing of harm has been made. A more expansive view of legitimate governance could result in a call for expensive studies in the light of such uncertainty to try to evaluate the danger, along with quarantines and other protective measures. If an industrial plant is the source of the substance, operations could be curtailed until more is known about the substance.

We find both impulses in our regulatory system. The bias in favor of protecting citizens from unknown, potential harms is reflected in the policy that requires FDA certification that new drugs are harmless before they can be put on the market. The bias in favor of no government interference, absent a demonstration of harm, is reflected in a legal system that requires the cleanup of dump sites only when a causal connection is established between the dumped materials and harmful consequences. A basic orientation toward the proper role of government affects budgetary priorities. Those who envision a more limited, only-prevent-harm-to-others role for government are often inclined to keep budgets smaller, deciding for example to spend less on an FDA budget line for inspecting food processing plants. Somewhat ironically, those who stress a role for government in preventing one person from harming another may be less likely to provide the resources required to determine whether such harm is actually occurring.

As a general matter, we should accept the reality of the unknown; we must accept the possibility of surprise. Unforeseen outcomes are inevitable. We should increase our collective willingness to "gamble" because we have no other choice. We take our chances every day, without being paralyzed in our decision making. We must act with incomplete and fallible knowledge. We know there will be mistakes. When we make those mistakes, we should learn from them, and move on. Acknowledging a policy world with no guarantees would mean finding ways to discourage institutionally the increasingly pervasive knee-jerk instinct to cast blame and find scapegoats for any time that policies do not achieve the desired effects. We have to empower decision makers to make good faith choices, knowing that sometimes they are going to be wrong. Unless there is evidence of bad faith, such inevitable "mistakes" should be viewed not as a fault for which decision makers bear liability, but as a reality of policy making and of the human condition itself.

We should also encourage flexible, adaptive, continually self-evaluating policy making institutions that are responsive to new information and changing circumstances. New policies should come with contingency planning in the form of built-in escape hatches that would allow an immediate alteration of a change in course to avoid the worst-case consequences. We should avoid ideological strait jackets that require the same response, decade after decade, even as what we know about the world—and the world itself—is dramatically changing.

Weighing options in light of uncertain futures leads to a range of possible operating principles: choose the policy alternative with the least-damaging worst-case scenario; choose the alternative that does no direct harm; weigh more heavily short-term costs and benefits, for which forecasts should be more accurate; avoid potential harms to our most vulnerable populations who are least able to offset losses, or to our most powerless populations, who are least able to muster political action to rectify mistakes. The world of policy making is a world of tradeoffs and compromises. Benefits are almost never secured without costs or risks of costs. The difficult question is how we can most effectively provide benefits and avoid harms, and it is this question to which we turn in the next chapter.

Notes

1 As one example, Louis Kaplow and Steven Shavell, in *Fairness Versus Welfare*, identify as their thesis the belief that "social decisions should be based *exclusively* on their effects on the welfare of individuals—and accordingly, should not depend on notions of fairness, justice or cognate concepts." *Fairness Versus Welfare* (Cambridge, MA: Harvard University Press, 2002), p. xvii.

2 A description of this program can be found in Dennis F. Thompson, *Political Ethics and Public Office* (Cambridge, MA: Harvard University Press, 1987), pp. 178–202.
3 Clifford Geertz, *The Interpretation of Cultures* (New York: Basic Books, 1973), pp. 28–9.
4 James Gleick, *Chaos: Making a New Science* (New York: Viking Press, 1987), p. 317.
5 For an excellent discussion of this issue, see the following exchange: William N. Trumbull, "Who Has Standing in Cost-Benefit Analysis?" *Journal of Policy Analysis and Management*, vol. 9, no. 2, 201–18 (1990); Dale Whittington and Duncan MacRae, Jr., "Comment: Judgments about Who Has Standing in Cost-Benefit Analysis," *Journal of Policy Analysis and Management*, vol. 9, no. 4, 536–47 (1990); William N. Trumbull, "Reply to Whittington and MacRae," *Journal of Policy Analysis and Management*, vol. 9, no. 4, 558–60 (1990).
6 The formative statement advocating for animal rights is Peter Singer's *Animal Liberation*, first published in 1975. The updated version is *Animal Rights: The Definitive Classic of the Animal Movement* (New York: HarperCollins, 2009). For a contrary view, see Peter Carruthers, *The Animals Issue: Moral Theory in Practice* (Cambridge: Cambridge University Press, 1992).
7 See Linda Kincaid, "Saving the Tuolumne," in Amy Gutmann and Dennis Thompson (eds.), *Ethics and Politics: Cases and Comments*, 4th ed. (Belmont, CA: ThomsonWadsworth, 2006), pp. 264–81.
8 David L. Weimer and Aidan R. Vining, *Policy Analysis: Concepts and Practice*, 4th ed. (Upper Saddle River, NJ: Prentice-Hall, 2005), p. 397.
9 W. Kip Viscusi and Joseph E. Aldy, "The Value of a Statistical Life: A Critical Review of Market Estimates Throughout the World," *The Journal of Risk and Uncertainty*, vol. 27, no. 1 (2003), pp. 5–76.
10 Elizabeth Anderson, *Value in Ethics and Economics* (Cambridge, MA: Harvard University Press, 1993), p. 197.
11 Peter Passell, "Disputed New Role for Polls: Putting a Price Tag on Nature," *The New York Times*, September 6, 1993, A-1.
12 An introductory discussion of four basic market failures (externalities, natural monopolies, information asymmetries, and public goods) can be found in Weimer and Vining, *Policy Analysis*, pp. 71–112. The authors also identify other obstacles to the efficient operation of a competitive market, such as the problem of uncertainty, thin markets, and macroeconomic dynamics (pp. 113–31).
13 Mark Sagoff, *The Economy of the Earth: Philosophy, Law and the Environment*, 2nd ed. (New York: Cambridge University Press, 2008), pp. 27–31.
14 Michael O'Hare and Debra Sanderson, "Facility Siting and Compensation: Lessons from the Massachusetts Experience," *Journal of Policy Analysis and Management*, vol. 12, no. 2 (1993), p. 370.
15 Paul R. Portney, "Trouble in Happyville," *Journal of Policy Analysis and Management*, vol. 11, no. 11 (1992), pp. 131–2.
16 Cass R. Sunstein, "Preferences and Politics," *Philosophy and Public Affairs*, vol. 20, no. 1 (Winter 1991), p. 11.
17 Michael Sandel, *What Money Can't Buy: The Moral Limits of Markets* (New York: Farrar, Strauss and Giroux, 2012), p. 7.

4 Stewardship of Resources
Effectiveness

Effectiveness is a moral value, rooted in a utilitarian understanding of ethics. A simple formulation of a utilitarian approach is that we should choose policy alternatives that produce the greatest net benefit. Those who govern have a moral obligation to be good stewards of public resources, to make effective use of those resources. The chapter on Benefit discussed how to identify, value and measure policy results. On the positive side of the ledger are benefits, goods and services. On the negative side are costs, harms and risks. While policy makers can usually identify the beneficial goals that they intend a policy to serve, the policy world is a world of tradeoffs. Benefits are rarely, if ever, secured without costs—often in the form of resources expended, restrictions on liberty, or loss of opportunities. We favor policies that not only produce benefits and avoid harms, but that do so in an effective way. After we have chosen ends that appear to offer benefits to the community, the search turns to the best means to achieve those ends.

Policy analysts have many tools at their disposal in their search for effective means, such as cost-benefit analysis, cost-effectiveness analysis, risk assessment, decision-tree methods, simulations and models, linear programming, game theory, and experimental trials. Rather than present these techniques in any depth, this chapter looks briefly at a few basic concepts to illustrate how policy effectiveness is assessed. Some clarity can be brought to the subject by looking at two kinds of tradeoffs: (1) those that focus on ends, and (2) those that focus on means. There are times when the effectiveness criterion is used primarily to select an appropriate policy end, and other times when the emphasis is on the most effective means to achieve an end that has already been chosen.

Tradeoffs among Outcomes

The strength of standard cost-benefit analysis (CBA) lies in the capacity of the technique to identify outcomes and measure tradeoffs among them. CBA can determine whether an end is worth pursuing (do costs exceed benefits?), and can rank different alternatives, if more than one option generates net benefits. The ideal policy would be one that produces a change in circumstances which improves the welfare of every affected party. Such a policy would satisfy the standard of Pareto improvement, by making some persons better off without making any others worse off. It is extremely rare to find public projects that meet the test of Pareto optimality, for such projects almost inevitably require the expenditure of funds (which are taken from some citizens through taxes) or at least the restriction of some persons' liberty. Even if the value of the gains of a project exceeds its losses, the Pareto principle would be satisfied only *if* the winners transferred enough of their gains to the losers so that they too would be no worse off. In the real world, however, such transfers are typically not mandated.

Policy analysts are more typically satisfied by applying the Kaldor-Hicks criterion[1] which requires that a net benefit be produced such that a transfer *could* be made which would make all affected parties at least as well off as they were before the implementation of the policy, with some even better off. It is sufficient that such a net gain could be produced, not that the benefits are actually distributed in this way. Thus the Kaldor-Hicks standard requires a *potential* Pareto outcome and is met when benefits exceed costs, even if the political will does not exist to make the transfers that would result in an actual Pareto improvement.

The calculation of relative gains and losses among different parties is complicated by the concept of declining marginal utility—a concept that suggests a presumptive bias toward the equal distribution of resources. The economic concept of declining marginal utility holds that the benefit that an individual receives from a specified unit of good decreases as the total amount of that good increases. This difference between exchange value (dollar value) and use value is illustrated by the difference in how $10,000 would be valued by Bill Gates and by a single mother living below the poverty line. The traditional understanding of diminishing marginal utility holds that, all else being equal, we would maximize the amount of existing total value if we distributed goods as evenly as possible among people, since a given amount of dollar value has greater use when it is used to obtain more of the goods that contribute to the well-being of their users.

The creation of winners and losers is a familiar issue that arises with a variety of public projects: think of the location of landfills, airports, and toxic waste dumps. These kinds of projects typically provide important benefits to the community at large, while also placing a large, disproportionate burden on those in the immediate vicinity of the siting. In an extremely oversimplified fashion, we could imagine the possible net outcomes of a proposed project being arrayed in a chart something like Table 4.1.

This chart reflects the outcomes of policy proposals which would have a differential effect on different populations, with those in the immediate impact area being affected less positively than those in the broader community. In the first three cases, the total net benefit of the program would be the same: 110 units. But the way in which those units of benefit are distributed reveals significant differences among the options. The fourth option

Table 4.1 Possible net outcomes of a proposed project

	Immediate area impact	Outside area impact	Combined impact
Option A	+10	+100	+110
Option B	−1	+111	+110
Option C	−50	+160	+110
Option D	−50	+60	+10

still theoretically produces a net benefit (10 units), but with an outcome that creates practical difficulties.

Option A results in something of a Pareto improvement outcome. All parties benefit (at least as aggregated in these two groups). Both those in the immediately impacted area and those in the broader community benefit from this option. Option B presents an outcome that would satisfy the concerns of the Kaldor-Hicks standard. There are losers; those in the immediate vicinity would be worse off, but it would be theoretically possible for the winners to make the transfer that would turn the outcome into a Pareto improvement. The same is true for Option C, but the burden imposed on the smaller group is so large that this alternative is more likely to create a Not-In-My-Backyard (NIMBY) problem. And, to press the point, while Option D formally meets the Kaldor-Hicks criteria, this kind of distribution of costs and benefits would almost certainly provoke NIMBY opposition.

Even when a project would create a large amount of net benefit, there are difficulties in moving to a Pareto efficient solution, especially in the case of projects which raise safety concerns. Providing compensation to local residents who view themselves as the losers is often viewed as a bribe—trading lives and health for money—unless the facility meets an acceptable threshold for safety. Thus, relatively few nuclear power plants have been built in the United States and only with great difficulty. Studies have concluded that merely providing monetary benefits to affected neighbors will do little to enhance the attractiveness of facilities that are perceived to be risky. In reality, such payments may even make the projects less acceptable to the affected residents. In the case of facilities that are viewed as more benign (e.g., landfills and prisons), using mechanisms other than distributing cash as a means of transferring some of the facility's benefits to local residents appears promising. Such mechanisms include providing improved health care services, guarantees against losses of property values, employment opportunities for community members, and charitable contributions to projects that are important to local residents. Another option has been to establish a contingency fund that serves as an insurance fund for the host community in the event of future accidents or other catastrophes. The existence of such a fund may be more important as a sign of confidence in the facility's safety than as contemplated revenue. These transfer mechanisms appear to be less useful for facilities that the public regards as particularly risky or of questionable legitimacy, such as radioactive waste repositories. In these cases, there is evidence that some mitigation measures, such as independent inspections and local ability to shut down a facility, may be more effective than monetary compensation.

The difficulty of evaluating the effectiveness of policies should not be underestimated. All of the problems just raised about measuring benefit apply to measuring costs. If anything, the problems of incommensurability are increased when we compare benefits with harms and costs. The public policy literature is full of stories that seem to give examples of instances in which those who were doing the math got the answer wrong. Justice Stephen Breyer has contributed this observation concerning a $9.3 million expenditure to remove "volatile organic compounds" from the dirt in the cleanup of a toxic waste dump in southern New Hampshire:

> How much extra safety did this $9.3 million buy? The forty-thousand-page record of this ten-year effort indicated (and all of the parties seemed to agree) that, without the extra expenditure, the waste dump was clean enough for children playing on the site to eat small amounts of dirt daily for 70 days each year without significant harm. Burning the soil would have made it clean enough for the children to eat small amounts daily for 245 days per year without significant harm. But there were no dirt-eating children playing in the area, for it was a swamp. Nor were dirt-eating children likely to appear there, for future building seemed unlikely. The parties also agreed that at least half of the volatile organic chemicals would likely evaporate by the year 2000.[2]

Because our community is often concerned about harms and benefits that are dear to us but difficult to quantify—such as human lives and health—we all too often read after-the-fact evaluations like Justice Breyer's. Some assessments of desirable ends fail the test of common sense. When doubts about our ability to accurately quantify benefits become so significant that cost-benefit analysis is of questionable utility, analysts can turn to cost-effectiveness analysis. This turn is one that moves the focus of effectiveness from ends to means.

Effective Means

Once policy makers have identified a desirable goal, the next step is to attempt to achieve that goal as efficiently as possible. Cost-effectiveness analysis is a method that attempts to identify effective means after the initial work of selecting ends has already been done. This approach focuses on attaining the benefit of a chosen policy goal at the lowest cost. Sometimes a decision has been made about policy goals to be pursued (such as reducing downtown traffic congestion by 20 percent, or increasing high school graduation rates by 10 percent), and the issue is how to achieve that goal at the least cost. Other times a decision has been made that a certain level of resources, say $1 billion, should be used for a particular purpose (such as improving health care services) and the task is to find the most effective way to spend that amount of money for that purpose. In either type of case, the focus is on finding the most efficient use of resources to achieve predetermined ends. Cost-effectiveness assessments, unlike cost–benefit analysis, do not require placing a monetary value on such intangible goods as human life, or levels of health, or clean air and water. This approach instead compares different policy alternatives by (1) evaluating the relative costs of options that produce a certain level of benefit, or (2) assessing the consequences of different options for using a specified amount of money.

In a landmark case that shaped environmental regulation, an opinion from the Fifth Circuit Court of Appeals[3] provides an illustration of how cost-effectiveness calculations have become a criterion to be used in policy making in the modern regulatory state. Beginning with the assumption that reducing deaths caused by cancer is a benefit, and responding to evidence that widespread and prolonged exposure to asbestos increases the number of deaths caused by cancer, the Environmental Protection Agency acted in 1989. The agency issued a rule under the Toxic Substances Control Act that prohibited the manufacture, importation, processing, and distribution of asbestos in almost all products. The rule was challenged on several grounds.

The Fifth Circuit Court of Appeals heard the case in the fall of 1991. At issue, among other matters, was the effectiveness of the EPA policy. The agency was required by statute to consider the costs of any proposed actions in a reasonable and prudent manner. The Court analyzed data provided by the agency and found that the bans on the use of various asbestos products would indeed save lives—but at a cost of $7 million to $106 million for each life saved. The Court concluded that the agency had violated the criterion of effectiveness. The judges rejected the EPA rules as ineffective because the projected cost per life saved through the implementation of this policy was much too high. The fault lay not in the choice of the desirable ends (preventing deaths) but in the use of means that were found to be ineffective.

Measuring the effectiveness of policies requires constant attention to difficult questions of tradeoff. How many cancer deaths a year per hundred thousand inhabitants are we willing to accept as we consider proposals to implement expensive toxic waste regulations? How do we decide, when debating clean air policy alternatives, that four cancer deaths per year in a region is too many, but one per year would be acceptable? How many HIV infections would need to be detected to justify costly and intrusive mandatory HIV-testing in order to obtain marriage licenses?

The American public is familiar with these distinctions between desirable ends and implementing effective means to achieve them. The debate about the Iraq War has been a prominent example. While some of the American public has continued to support the ends the war was intended to achieve, it has become difficult to find any public voices that consider the means used in the first few years of the conflict to be effective ones.

A good example of an effort to adopt effective means can be drawn from the actions of the city of New London, Connecticut that led to the Supreme Court's ruling in *Kelo v. City of New London* in 2005.[4] In 2000, the city of New London approved a development plan that was projected to create more than 1,000 jobs, increase tax revenues, and revitalize the city's downtown and waterfront areas. The city council authorized the New London Development Corporation (NLDC), a private nonprofit entity, to purchase property or to acquire property by exercising eminent domain in the city's name. The NLDC succeeded in negotiating the purchase of most of the real estate in the 90-acre project area, but when initial negotiations failed with a few remaining land owners, the NLDC initiated condemnation proceedings. Nine landowners went to court.

The decision to pursue eminent domain proceedings was a decision based on effectiveness. The option of continuing negotiation would have come with high transaction costs and the prospect of higher purchasing costs. That approach would have been time-consuming and, if mutually agreeable prices could be found, expensive. Further, there was no guarantee that the negotiations route would have been successful at all. Condemning the property, and then taking it, offered the prospect of a more efficient path. Of course, five years of litigation dramatically affected the cost-effectiveness of choosing this route to reach the desired ends.

A final ingredient in assessing the effectiveness of means is a dose of reality. Policies that may play out well in on-paper exercises may, in the end, be ineffective simply because on-the-ground realities would not allow their implementation. We simply can't do everything we might want to do. This kind of reality check is a significant factor in the current debate on immigration policy. Some American citizens are advocating the deportation of 12 million illegal immigrants, but considerable doubt exists about whether it would even be possible to deport 12 million undocumented residents— never mind the cost. Our policy choices are always constrained by the realities of our circumstances, no matter how far they may be from our normative ideals.

Effectiveness and Popular Control

Effectiveness runs head on into a fundamental political value. Two basic issues that loom over the policy-making process are (1) how to make policies more effective in solving social problems, and (2) how to insure that policy making is responsive to popular control. Abraham Lincoln gave voice to our aspiration that our government be a government "of the people, by the people, for the people." The most effective policy apparatus, in the right hands, will give us government *for* the people. But, if we want government *of* and *by* the people, the cause of effectiveness will be compromised.

At times, there is a direct conflict between popular control of the policy process and the effectiveness with which policy goals can be achieved. We are often willing to make such a tradeoff because one operating premise of a government like ours is that we need government of and by the people in order to increase the chance that the policy apparatus *will* be in the right hands.

There are times when the active role played by a misinformed public has resulted in flawed decisions, with resources and regulation being employed that are disproportionate to the risk of harms being avoided. At times, it seems that the greater the public's role in influencing calculations of effectiveness, the less likely we are to create policy that is appropriately effective. The answer, according to this line of thought, is to give greater power to regulatory agencies, which are more likely to respond to scientific experts than to public misperceptions. If these decisions are removed from the political process, we could arguably be able to achieve assessments of effectiveness that more accurately reflect scientifically objective measures of harm and risk of harm.

This removal of some calculations from the political process could be defended as giving the public what it should want, or what it "really" wants—rather than what the public says it wants. However, too heavy a reliance on scientific experts, especially when their judgment conflicts with what appears to be a public consensus, raises a number of questions— particularly in a democracy. One purpose of allowing the experts to make the decisions is to fashion policy that will, in fact, provide the benefits the public wants in the most effective manner. However, it is not at all clear that a body of scientific experts, particularly those in charge of a government agency, will be insulated from non-scientific pressures. "Capture" of regulatory bureaucracies by the regulated communities is a real possibility—as has become clear in the aftermath of the 2010 BP oil spill in the Gulf of Mexico. Such bureaucracies develop their own interests that influence the way they identify problems, frame issues, and propose solutions. The personal values and opinions of experts inevitably affect the design of their work and the conclusions they reach.

This tension between effectiveness and popular control is regularly played out in our halls of government. Sunshine laws and open meeting laws are passed, and governing officials promptly look for ways to get around them or diminish their reach. The concern of policy makers is that too much openness, too many restrictions on behind-closed-doors conversations and deliberations, will create obstacles to effective policy making. Two high-profile cases demonstrate the tug and pull of this policy making issue.

In 2001, newly-inaugurated President George W. Bush created a National Energy Policy Development Group that was chaired by Vice-President Richard Cheney. The task force was charged with making recommendations to the President on the nation's energy policy. Despite repeated requests and demands from many quarters, the Bush administration refused to identify the members of the group, or provide information about the task force meetings—such as who attended, the time and place of the meetings, or the grounds on which participants were selected. Eight years earlier, newly-inaugurated President Bill Clinton created a task force on National Health Care Reform that was chaired by his wife, Hillary Clinton. The task force was charged with preparing health care reform legislation. All of the meetings of the task force, except one, were closed to the public, and numerous subsequent requests for information about the workings of the task force were denied.

In each case, the defense of this secrecy was couched in the same terms that have generally justified claims of Executive privilege over the years. Public scrutiny, we were told, would compromise the President's ability to receive advice that was crucial to carrying out his responsibilities in an effective way. Conducting business in public view would have a chilling effect on the President's interaction with his advisors. These administrators would be less forthcoming, making it more difficult for the Executive branch to get the valuable, candid advice and information upon which good decision making depends.

We certainly want our leaders to act on the basis of the "best" advice they can get. One question is whether secret interactions increase or decrease the quality of that advice. Clearly part of the demand for more openness in the cases of both of these task forces was a fear that each had been captured by special interest groups. And, while secrecy no doubt facilitates the flow of some types of information, it also undermines accountability in the political process. Accountability requires a considerable degree of transparency in government. If one of our goals as a nation is to maintain a government that is accountable to the people and responsive to their will, secrecy undermines efforts to effectively achieve that goal. Certainly there are cases in which interest in government openness is overridden by other interests—the cause of national security in time of war being the most obvious of such cases.

Even when our focus is with only the effectiveness of our policy making, we should approach with caution any calls for reducing the public's participation in the political process. In this regard, a parallel can be drawn with the legal prohibition of monopolies in a free-enterprise capitalist system. While monopolies might be the result of one company's provision of the greatest benefit for consumers in the short run, monopolies are prohibited because the governing conviction is that in the longer term a greater benefit will be secured for the community by preventing the formation of monopolies. Similarly, short-term efficiencies in policy making at the expense of public accountability may well lead to long-term losses in effectiveness. A monopoly of political power (which is created by limiting knowledge) is likely to not only violate values of responsiveness and accountability, but also to produce less effective government in the long run.

Another effectiveness issue arises in the difference between the opinions and preferences of the lay people that comprise the general public and the opinions and preferences of experts—whether they be scientists, government officials or political professionals. There do appear to be differences between how the public assesses risk and harms and how they are often assessed by experts. In the public mind it is often important, to a degree not usually reflected in scientific assessment, whether the risks citizens are asked to bear are voluntary, hidden, unknowable, novel, uncontrollable, catastrophic, inequitable, or especially painful. Some scientists or policy analysts may want to dismiss some of these public perceptions as "irrational" or "misinformed." However, to the extent the expert judgments about public perceptions are correct, the slow, tedious and often frustrating task of public education may be preferable to ignoring popular sentiments.

A traditional top-down process of command-and-control or announce-and-defend could be replaced, or at least moderated, with a more decentralized collaborative process. This shift addresses a concern that technical risk assessment or CBA analysis brings an undeserved aura of assurance or scientific legitimacy to political decisions that are inescapably value-laden. While the quantitative approaches may appear to further an efficient expenditure of resources, they may narrow the focus of the inquiry to the point that they miss significant concerns (moral, socioeconomic, political) that escape technocratic analysis.

There is not a simple solution to the experts-versus-the-lay-public debate. Different decisions call for different levels of deference to experts and for different levels of public involvement. We can construct a continuum: at one end is a model which places virtually all control in the hands of scientists and other experts; at the other end is a model which leaves the decision to the public, perhaps through a referendum. The first model works best for highly technical, implementation processes, where policy decisions require a level of expertise far beyond the reach of even an educated lay public, and where those decisions are made within the bounds of clearly-articulated public goals, probably expressed through enabling legislation. The second model works best for those decisions based on fundamental principles, where policy should be directed by some choice between differing, basic societal priorities. Even at these extremes the two communities of decision-makers are not isolated from one another, and most policy-making processes will fall somewhere in the middle of the continuum.

A case that illustrates the challenges of finding the right place on the continuum between effectiveness and popular control is an episode in policy making concerning the now-defunct Asarco copper smelter in Ruston, Washington.[5] In 1983, the Environmental Protection Agency announced proposed standards that would regulate arsenic emissions from copper smelting and glass manufacturing plants in the United States. The standards were expected to have their greatest impact around Tacoma, Washington, where the nation's only copper smelter that used ore with high arsenic content was operated by the American Smelting and Refining Company (ASARCO).

The proposed regulations applied the best available technology to reduce emissions, but only to a level that might still result in about one additional cancer death per year among Tacoma-area residents. Imposing the higher standards to eliminate that residual risk could have made the plant uneconomical to operate. EPA administrator William Ruckelshaus proposed involving the public in the process of deciding how stringent the regulations should be. He characterized the issue as "what risks are we willing to take and for what benefit?"

The decision to involve the public in the standards-setting process raised several issues. Ruckelshaus indicated that EPA would be actively soliciting the views and wishes of the residents who lived and worked near the ASARCO smelter because they would be most affected by the regulations. Yet, EPA was setting nation-wide standards, standards that would affect Americans across the country. Indeed, the EPA was acting in response to a U.S. District Court ruling in a case involving the state of New York and a glass manufacturing plant in New Jersey.

Even within the Tacoma area, "the public" was not a homogenous monolith. The smelter was located in the small company town of Ruston (population of 636) where it employed 575 workers. The citizens of Ruston depended on the plant for their livelihood. Differently situated were: the residents of Tacoma, who received tons of air pollutants annually from the plant; the people living two miles offshore on Vashon Island who were worried about high levels of arsenic in their soil and in their children's urine samples; and the fishermen trying to make their living in Commencement Bay—which had already been designated as a Superfund clean-up site, partially because of accumulated arsenic on the bottom of the bay.

If the public is to be involved in policy processes of this sort, should the residents around Tacoma have a greater say than citizens in other parts of the country—because the impact on them would be greater? Within the Tacoma area, should the residents of Ruston have a greater say—again, because the impact on them would be greater? When the public hearings were held in the Tacoma area, what purpose should they have been serving? Arguably one concern that should have guided EPA decision making was the legislature's intent when the Clean Air Act was passed. But that is not the kind of matter that is usually resolved in community meetings. An EPA spokesperson told reporters, "Together we must determine 'what is an "acceptable" or "reasonable" risk to public health from arsenic emissions.' " To one observer, that sounded like "asking people how much cancer they would like to have." On the other hand, as Ruckelshaus noted when responding to criticism about the way citizens were being involved in the process, "What's the alternative? Don't involve them? Then you're accused of doing something nefarious."

In the end, this discussion circles back to the nature of a representative democracy. Between the polar opposites of a participatory democracy on one end of the continuum and a regulatory state on the other is our representative democracy in which policy is ultimately made by the representatives who attempt to take into account both public preferences and expert knowledge. There will be times when a government actor will make a decision because it reflects the perceived will of her constituency. There will be other times when a government actor will make a decision because the best information available has convinced her that it will serve the common good, even if the action is contrary to the perceived will of her constituency. There is no clear standard that tells our policy makers when it is appropriate to make one choice or the other. This is not a new problem, but the increasingly complex and sophisticated information that is needed to inform policy choices makes it a more serious one.

Limitations on the Reach of Effectiveness

A prominent feature in the calculation of the effectiveness of policy proposals is estimating the magnitude of risk to people from exposure to various situations. Risk assessment is a tool that is used to evaluate the size of the risk that particular harms will result from policy options that are being studied. Policy makers are almost always making decisions based on projections of future effect, but they can never see the future perfectly. So, instead of trading off benefits that are certain, against costs and harms that are known, policy makers are usually balancing the probability that particular consequences will result from given actions.

The front pages of our newspapers are full of stories that implicate policy making based on risk assessment, stories about guarding against terrorism, airplane hijackings and inspecting shipping containers; food and drug safety; building protection from hurricanes and floods and coping with climate change. Our national debate over the expansion of our nuclear power capacity contains particularly enlightening stories about risk assessment because the processes are so complex and the perceived risks of harm are so great. As interest in cleaner sources of energy has increased in recent years, discussions about the risks associated with the development of nuclear power plants have taken on a new urgency.

In the spring of 2013, the Nuclear Regulatory Commission concluded that all but five of the nation's 104 nuclear reactors were performing at acceptable safety levels at the end of 2012. "The performance is quite good," reported the Commission's chairman, while also noting that you can't have that many reactors up and running without having "a few that are going to have difficulty." The Union of Concerned Scientists reacted by issuing its own report which stated that nearly a sixth of the reactors experienced safety breaches in that calendar year. The breaches, they reported, were due in part to weak oversight, a laxness that could have been fed by the Commission's "tolerating the intolerable." How can two different groups, acting in good faith, come to such diametrically opposed conclusions? The answer to that question is rooted in the complex and unknowable factors that drive risk assessments.

The events at the Three Mile Island Unit (TMI) near Middletown, Pennsylvania, in 1979, have served as a laboratory for enhancing our understanding of the risk assessment process.[6] On March 28, the main feed-water pumps stopped running at TMI, as a result of either a mechanical or electrical failure, which prevented the steam generators from removing heat. In order to prevent the heat buildup from causing excessive pressure, a relief valve was opened, but the valve did not close automatically when it should have. Signals to the operators failed to show that the valve was still open; as a result, cooling water poured out of the valve that was stuck open, causing the core of the reactor to overheat. Operators received confusing information from instruments and incorrectly assumed that the core was properly covered with coolant. When alarms rang and warning lights flashed, the operators thus took a series of actions that made the conditions worse by reducing the flow of coolant through the core. About one-half of the core melted.

A combination of personnel error, design deficiencies and component failure was blamed for the incident. A fact sheet from the U.S. Nuclear Regulatory Commission reports that two and three days after the initial incident there was still "a great deal of confusion and consternation," "growing uncertainty," "new worries," and "great anxiety." At that time, there was still concern about a breach of containment. This feature of the report should give us pause. If the outcome of this incident was still in doubt three days *after* these events, we should approach risk assessments for the distant future with some humility.

These are precisely the concerns that have been addressed in a number of studies on nuclear reactor safety. One such study of the potential hazards of commercial nuclear reactors was funded by the Nuclear Regulatory Commission in the 1970s, prior to the Three Mile Island incident. The Rasmussen Commission (the group was chaired by MIT nuclear engineering professor Norman Rasmussen) conducted an extensive study, at a cost of $4 million, to assess the risks posed by the construction and operation of reactors.

The purpose of the study was to estimate risks. A review of what was not included in the scope of the study, however, raises questions about how useful the report's estimate could be, because some topics were beyond the commission's charter. The commissioners were instructed not to address terrorist sabotage, theft and natural disasters, or long-term effects on health. They did not consider related issues such as the disposal of nuclear waste and the decommissioning of plants at the end of their useful lives. The commission also did not address human error. The report did not include any calculation of the risks and effects of operator error of the sort found in the Three Mile Island incident. (Many of the actions taken by operators at TMI made the situation worse than it might have been.) While these limitations on the scope of the commission's work may have been necessary for the study to be manageable, the conclusions could hardly be considered comprehensive.

Another nuclear plant example demonstrates how an almost infinite number of possible future events, and interactions among those events, renders any certainty about predictions illusory:

> The crippling 1975 fire at the Browns Ferry plant in Alabama was touched off by an electrician's holding a candle up to a seal in a wall (in violation of standard procedure) to check for an air leak, which ignited the temporary sealant he had just patched the wall with, which smoldered through into the wall space, which then burned the plastic insulation off reactor control wiring that, in bad design, passed through the space alongside the two emergency backup cables, and led to such havoc as knocking out control systems and sending acrid smoke and fire-extinguisher carbon dioxide into the control room: much damage was done, and the accident was extremely threatening.[7]

Event Tree Analysis is a technique that is often used to assess the probability of a safety hazard. An event tree starts with a potential undesired event, and follows possible further system events through to a series of final consequences. The analysis begins with hypothetical Event A, then projects the consequences (Events A1, A2, A3 . . .) that could flow from that initial event, then projects the possible consequences that could flow from each of those second order events, and so forth. As the number of events increases, the chart fans out like the branches of a tree. Probabilities for all of the different outcomes are calculated as each event is added to the analysis. Another technique, Fault Tree Analysis, works in just the opposite way, beginning with an undesired final consequence and then working backward through all of the potential events that could conceivably lead to that final result.

Thus, for an event tree analysis to have successfully projected the probability of the Browns Ferry incident, the analyst would have to have estimated the probability that a worker would have used a candle to check for an air leak, then the probability that the candle would have ignited a temporary sealant, then the probability that the ignited sealant would have smoldered through into the wall space, and so forth. Similarly, a valid assessment of the probability of the Three Mile Island incident would have calculated, in turn, the likelihood that the feedwater pumps would fail, that the relief valve would fail to close properly, that automated signals would fail to notify operators of the valve's failure, etc.

Event tree analysis was used, after the fact, as BP attempted to analyze what went wrong on its Deepwater Horizon rig. A string of multiple failures was identified in its September, 2010, Accident Investigation Report:

1   Cement was pumped down the production casing to prevent hydro-carbons from entering the wellbore annulus, but mistakes in cement design, testing and quality assurance led to a failure that allowed the hydrocarbons to enter the annulus.

2   The hydrocarbons were then able to pass down the wellbore and enter the production casing, because both barriers in a shoe track that was designed to prevent this entry failed.

3   The rig crew and well site leaders incorrectly read the results of a test, and thus failed to understand that the shoe track barrier was flawed.

4   The flow of hydrocarbons increased as operations continued because the rig crew failed to recognize the influx.

5 and 6 The first well control actions routed fluids to the mud gas separator system, rather than overboard, and the hydrocarbons were then vented directly onto the rig (apparently due to a design flaw), which increased the possibility of the gas reaching an ignition source.

7   The heating, ventilation and air conditioning system probably trans-ferred a gas-rich mixture into the engine rooms, further increasing the potential of ignition.

8   Three different methods for operating the blowout preventer failed to seal the well: (a) the emergency disconnect system was likely disabled by the explosions and fire; (b) both a fault in a critical solenoid valve, and an insufficient charge in control batteries prevented the activation of an automatic emergency sealing function; and (c) a remotely operated blind shear ram failed to seal the well.

A comprehensive event tree analysis would begin with a listing of all initial events that are likely (as likely as the worker's use of the candle or the failure of the feedwater pumps) to set off a chain of events that would lead to problems. The most difficult part of conducting a thorough event tree analysis is accounting for and establishing probabilities for all sorts of human error. Some assessments explicitly exclude human error. But, it seems likely that a low estimate of risk, based on little or no probability being assigned to human error, will increase the possibility of human error. How alert will an operator be to a developing series of events when she has been told that those events have about as much chance of occurring as being struck by a meteor (a conclusion drawn in the Rasmussen study)? Apparently, one of the reasons for the delay in reacting to the *Exxon Valdez* accident in order to contain the oil spill in Prince William Sound was that a risk assessment had projected that one such accident would occur every 241 years. In the context of this assessment, the managers did not initially believe that the *Exxon Valdez* incident was as serious as early reports were saying that it was. Early reports on the BP oil spill indicated that BP and other oil companies had based their plans for responding to an oil spill on faulty data—on U.S. government projections that assigned very low odds to the probability of oil reaching shorelines, even in the case of a spill that was larger than this one was. The result, an almost inevitable result, was inadequate contingency planning to deal with the consequences of an event such as the one that occurred.

Risk analysts face a daunting challenge in attempting to place a probability on a series of events that has never been observed. There is a difference between probability and uncertainty. Risk assessments in the area of highway safety can produce reliable probabilities, given the experience and voluminous data that have been accumulated over the years. Assessments of unprecedented events inevitably involve projections that entail calculations that are more like guesswork. These concerns apply not only to risk assessment, but to cost-benefit analysis, cost-effectiveness analysis, and similar assessment tools. The point is not that these assessments are useless, but that we must keep the reliability of such assessments in perspective. Any analysis of highly complex operations, no matter how intensive the effort may be, will be inherently of limited utility. Our task is to decide how to respond to these shortcomings, to decide what reliance should be placed on these types of studies.

Making Policy with Imperfect Information

Given the inevitable weaknesses in any efforts to project the effectiveness of just about any policy, how should we proceed? First, we should not stop doing risk assessment, cost-benefit, or other kinds of quantitative analysis. We should not allow some unattainable standard of perfection to become the enemy of the best studies that we are capable of producing. Of course, we should work to improve the process, to refine the instruments and adjust the models in light of new experiences and information. The value of assessments is also enhanced when those who conduct them are upfront and explicit about where the estimates are guesswork, which choices are value-based, and which conclusions are subject to dispute and disagreement by other investigators.

These studies are typically technical and full of numbers and equations. That appearance should not be used to mask uncertainty. Surely the experts who possess the expertise and mounds of data, and have experience in using these methods, will be tempted to over-claim for their results—especially when they find themselves criticized by a skeptical but uninformed public. A better response would be a candid acknowledgement of shortcomings. Highlighting the places where there is uncertainty rather than probability, or pointing to controversy and disagreement among experts, may appear to devalue the studies and the standing of the experts. But, in the longer run, all of these caveats and disclaimers are important, as they help prevent the shortcomings of the less solid and less certain exercises from unduly undermining the studies that are on firmer ground.

A corollary to this first point is the importance of news media and other organizations acknowledging these caveats as they pass along the information. Few individuals read these reports. Most of us encounter their content through mediating institutions and professionals. These mediators bear an important responsibility to not skip over the disclaimers for the sake of simplicity or attention-grabbing headlines. And what is important for the media is doubly important for politicians whose point scoring is often reduced when uncertainties in findings are acknowledged.

Second, careful thought needs to be given to the way politics and values affect the use of the information generated by these assessments. A recent example of the way that basic values affect the impact of risk assessment in the policy arena is the European Union's implementation in the summer of 2008 of new restrictions on the makers of chemicals that might be linked to cancer and other health problems. The new laws require companies to demonstrate that a chemical is safe before it enters commercial markets. Just the opposite policy is in place in the United States, where regulators must prove that a chemical is harmful before it can be restricted or removed from the market. This difference reflects fundamental differences in values related to the nature and scope of government, regulation, and free enterprise. This value difference is not trivial, as U.S. manufacturers estimated that the new European regulations would add billions of dollars to their costs. At least one piece of the conversation should move beyond established ideological biases to ask which governmental response is more appropriate, given the nature of the information available to policy makers in these particular cases.

Once we think we know something about the probabilities of the outcomes of various scenarios, decisions must be made about how to incorporate those findings into the public policy process. Do we manage to the most probable outcome? Do we make policy to avoid the worst case scenario, or to attempt to achieve the best case scenario? Such questions are best answered not in the abstract, but should be tailored to concrete cases. Evidence-based policy making has become the new touchstone for good governance. At the very least, this approach emphasizes the need to look at the facts on the ground, in each place where they are encountered, rather than relying on ideological reactions that have been passed down from other times and other places.

A third consideration in making policy responses to these kinds of studies relates to particular features of risk assessment analysis, including the use of contingent valuation and discount rates, opportunity costs, and intrinsic values. The uncertainty we encounter about the basic data that drive much policy analysis must be addressed. Earlier, we discussed the understandable suspicion of results that contingent valuation techniques yield in the context of cost-benefit analysis. Another matter of concern is the wildly varying results that flow from using different discount rates. Policy analysts routinely use discount rates to determine the present value of future benefits. The reasonableness of this technique is reflected in the fact that people generally value a dollar in the present more than the promise of the same amount of money at some future date. However, the choice of what discount rate to use (in essence, predicting a kind of future inflation rates) exerts a significant impact on the conclusions that are reached. Very different answers are produced, depending on which rate is chosen.

Consider, for example, the future value of a benefit that is worth $100 today when different discount rates are used to estimate benefits and costs one hundred years into the future. Using a 3 percent discount rate, the future value of that $100 is $5.20. But if a 5 percent rate is used, the value decreases to only 76 cents; while a 1 percent rate calculation yields a value of $36.97. It is not unusual for the outcome of a cost-benefit analysis of a proposed policy to depend on the discount rate that is used. Since the choice of a discount rate has such a dramatic effect on the assessment of policy options, and since no one knows what a reliable estimate of future inflation is, it is no wonder that skepticism and disbelief characterize some responses to such studies. This skepticism and disbelief are aggravated by the all too common experience of finding experts with one political bent using high discount rates, while experts on the other side of the political divide use low discount rates on the same question.

Opportunity costs pose another challenge that must be addressed. These represent the value of opportunities that are forgone when resources are spent on any given program—e.g., allocating a parcel of land for one use, rather than for other competing possibilities. A full accounting of opportunity costs would, theoretically, require a comparative analysis of every possible alternative use of those resources—clearly an impossible ideal to meet. This difficulty of measuring one outcome against all future options (options that can only be imagined) creates a caveat that should accompany any "complete" assessment. The stakes are heightened in the cases of policy actions that are irreversible.

Finally, the use of conclusions from effectiveness studies should take place in the context of the reminder that there are values which are beyond the scope of those types of analysis, at least as they are traditionally understood. Effectiveness is an instrumental value. Efficiency can serve evil ends. The management of the concentration camps in the Third Reich may well have been an efficient way to carry out the Nazi program of genocide. But sometimes we don't want the trains to run on time. A focus on effectiveness should not obscure an evaluation of the goals being served, and some kinds of values are not as amenable to the tradeoffs of efficiency analysis as others.

There are limits to how freely we want to trade off items of intrinsic value. Returning to the discussion about the way we value nature, it is certainly possible to use quantitative methods to evaluate projects that alter the natural world. We've discussed the alternate assessments of a project to build dams on the Tuolumne River in California—assessments that included projections of the production of electricity, recreational use of the alternative configurations of the river, and option value estimates of non-users' interest in maintaining existing conditions. Analysts were focusing on costs and benefits to humans, in deciding the fate of this natural area.

Here is another approach to valuing natural resources: "The earth is a living, conscious being. In company with cultures of many different times and places, we name these things as sacred: air, fire, water, and earth. . . . To call these things sacred is to say that they have a value beyond their usefulness for human ends, that they themselves become the standards by which our acts, our economies, our laws, and our purposes must be judged."[8] In this kind of statement we encounter a Kantian-type affirmation that nature should be treated as an end and not merely as a means to achieve other ends. This conviction rejects an objectifying of the natural world which leads us to see her as only a means for achieving economic profit or serving the pleasure of humans. Some policymakers and citizens may not be persuaded to join in this sentiment. But that is a decision that should be made deliberately, as we are constantly mindful of the nature of the ends that are being served by effective means.

Behavioral Economics: The Endowment Effect

One aspect of the way we value costs and benefits is the reality known as the endowment effect. People value gains and losses differently, placing more weight on losses than gains. Experiments have regularly shown that individuals value a good that they already own more than they would pay to obtain that same good. This disparate valuation is called the endowment effect because the difference appears at the time that a person is endowed with ownership rights. This concept not only describes yet another complicating factor in our efforts to understand how humans value benefits and harms in the real world, but also points us to the discussions of Fairness and Fidelity that follow.

Behavioral economics is the study of humans in the marketplace. While traditional economic analysis is often conducted with theoretical models based on idealized rational actors, behavioral economics analyzes the choices humans actually make—with all of their information deficits, short attention spans, emotional responses and self-control issues. The focus is on empirical evidence about what people do, rather than models of what self-interested rational actors should do. Among the contributions behavioral economics has made to the world of policy making is demonstrating the operation of the endowment effect.

Behavioral economics studies consistently demonstrate that people routinely place a higher value on losses than on "equal" gains; they value a good or service that they already have more than they value that identical good or service when it is contemplated as something they could gain. These findings are reported from an array of survey studies, real exchange experiments, and the choices individuals make in their daily lives. People demand greater compensation to give up a good than they would be willing to pay to acquire it—sometimes two to five times as much. This reality appears to be a pervasive characteristic of individuals' preferences, and it does not appear to be related to income, wealth constraints, or transactions costs.

The existence of the endowment effect has important implications for the kind of economic models that are used to assess benefit and harm. For instance, the amount that a group of citizens would be willing to pay to clean up a waste site is not likely to be the same as the compensation they would be willing to accept in order to allow someone to pollute the site in the first place. While the data from many controlled tests have consistently shown that losses matter more to people than gains, the working practice of many economists and policy analysts has been to assume an equivalence between Willingness to Pay and Willingness to Accept Payment valuations. When a measure like Willingness to Pay is used to measure a cost (rather than the Willingness to Accept Payment for a loss), the magnitude of losses or harms can be seriously understated because of the endowment effect.

Some analysts consider the actual choices that deviate from rational choice models to be irrational mistakes or biases, and thus do not take them into account for the purposes of assessing effectiveness. In these cases, the evidence that has accumulated about the real world is ignored, and an analysis of the effectiveness of a policy proceeds based on theoretical constructs. If, on the other hand, an analyst thinks that these revealed differences in individuals' valuations should be incorporated into assessments of policies, then a number of inferences can be drawn from the endowment effect. One of these is that existing distributions are very important. This built-in bias toward the status quo enhances the importance of the existing allocations of goods and services, and casts doubt on the belief that free market exchanges can be relied upon to overcome initial unequal distributions.[9] This status quo bias creates a significant barrier to movement toward arrangements that are fairer or that create a greater overall utility in a community. Public policy that ignores or denies the inequalities that are built into many social settings reinforces the power structures in which people that have power tend to keep it, while those without power face stiff headwinds in efforts to obtain it.

A second set of implications is related to actions that impose losses on particular parties or groups—the kind of policies that create NIMBY (Not-In-My-Backyard) type circumstances. People often prefer reductions in imposed harms over comparable amounts of compensation for suffering those harms. The use of money to pay off the "losers" in a transaction, as a means of making them whole or eliminating opposition to development projects, may be an ineffective and expensive strategy—especially when compared to options that reduce the magnitude of the loss in the first instance.

Some researchers have characterized this variation in valuation as an irrational overvaluing of the status quo. But for those who want policy to reflect revealed preferences, it is important to recognize and to respond to valuations in the real market, not some imagined "ideal" market in which forgoing a given amount of benefit is considered to be equivalent to obtaining the same amount of benefit.

Scientists and social scientists have failed to come to a consensus about how to account for the endowment effect. From an ethical point of view, these realities appear to have something to do with what people think they are entitled to, with what they think they deserve. The bottom line is that individuals think they have a right to keep what they have. Thus the Willingness-to-Accept value of the loss of a good can be thought of as being equal to the Willingness-to-Pay value to obtain the good, *plus* a premium for giving up that right. Similarly, risk aversion can be thought of as a way of avoiding the loss of what one deserves—the risk that exists in any exchange of not being treated fairly and getting what one is entitled to in return. Consider a proposed budget revision that would take $100 million from one constituency and give it to another. In reality, this would be difficult to accomplish; those who lose would object more strenuously than the winners would argue for it. The judgment that policy makers have to make is whether this is a reality that should receive ethical notice, or only a fact of life that should be set aside as best as possible in constructing ethical policy recommendations.

There are two non-consequentialist notions that explain granting the kind of weight to the status quo that is reflected in the endowment effect. First, the policy maker should recognize distinctive obligations that may arise in existing relationships. A relationship exists between the government actors and those currently receiving government benefits or services. A change in policy that would remove existing benefits may be seen as violating responsibilities that have been incurred. The point is not that withdrawal of the benefits can never be justified, but that there may well be an established relationship that requires a greater justification than would be required, for example, in deciding not to provide new benefits of the same value to a different group. There seems to be something here, other than inertia or political expediency, which counts against removing a benefit. Viewing the matter from the perspective of the current receivers of a benefit, the existence of the status quo can be seen as a source of special entitlement. The benefit may have been "possessed" for so long that the recipients have come to rely on it. This does not make the entitlement one that cannot be overridden by other considerations, but additional justification may be required to present a persuasive case that the change is desirable. In this light, it is not surprising that none of the Social Security reforms that are on the table propose dramatic changes for current recipients in the program.

This second feature of right or entitlement can be seen more clearly when what is being taken away from someone is not something they are receiving from the government but something which they have come to possess by some other means. What kind of entitlement does someone have to the money she has earned or won in a lottery when increased taxes are being considered? What kind of right does someone have to a piece of land he has inherited when he faces losing it through eminent domain for use for the public good? What kind of entitlement does someone have to one of her kidneys when it is needed to save the life of a fellow citizen?

Issues of justice, fairness and desert complicate any simple balancing of costs and benefits. The endowment effect may reflect some intuitive sense that calculating the value of benefits to be granted and costs to be borne, without taking account of existing relationships and entitlements, doesn't answer all of our questions. In the next chapter we will explore some of these additional considerations, as we move from consequentialist-laden considerations of Benefit and Effectiveness to the non-consequentialist concerns included in the benchmarks of Fairness and Fidelity.

Notes

1 Named after Nicholas Kaldor ("Welfare Propositions of Economics and Interpersonal Comparisons of Utility," *Economic Journal*, 49 (1939), 549–52), and John R. Hicks ("The Foundation of Welfare Economics," *Economic Journal*, 49 (1939), 697–712).
2 Stephen Breyer, *Breaking the Vicious Circle* (Cambridge, MA: Harvard University Press, 1993), p. 12.
3 Corrosion Proof Fittings v. Environmental Protection Agency, 947 F.2d 1201 (5th Cir. 1991).
4 545 U.S. 469 (2005).
5 The facts presented here are drawn from Esther Scott, "The Risks of Asarco," in Amy Gutmann and Dennis Thompson (eds.), *Ethics and Politics: Cases and Comments*, 4th ed. (Belmont, CA: Thomson Wadsworth, 2006. Copyright: Case Program, Kennedy School of Government, Harvard University).
6 The source for the description of this incident is "Three Mile Island Accident," a fact sheet of the Office of Public Affairs, United States Nuclear Regulatory Commission. (*www.nrc.gov/reading-rm/doc-collections/fact-sheets/3mile-isle.html*) (last reviewed/updated February 11, 2013)
7 William W. Lawrence, *Modern Science and Human Values* (New York: Oxford University Press, 1985), p. 144.
8 Starhawk, *The Fifth Sacred Thing*, (New York: Bantam Books, 1994), frontispiece.
9 Jack L. Knetsch, "Policy Analysis and Design with Losses Valued More than Gains and Varying Rates of Time Preferences," in *Judgments, Decisions and Public Policy*, Rajeer Gowand and Jeffrey C. Fox (eds.) (Cambridge: Cambridge University Press, 2002), pp. 92–3.

5 Serving Justice

Fairness

As we've discussed in the chapters on Benefit and Effectiveness, we want to know that a policy, or proposed policy, effectively produces a societal benefit. But we need to know more to approve of that policy. It is not enough that a policy passes a cost-benefit test. We want to believe that a policy is fair. At a general level, fairness means giving people what they are due, what they deserve. It means that they are treated equitably, without prejudice or bias. Like cases are treated alike. Fairness requires that goods and services (as well as costs, burdens and risks) be distributed fairly.

Sometimes fairness is used to judge the way an individual is treated. Did she receive proper compensation for the taking of her land? Sometimes, especially in the public policy arena, fairness concerns are applied to a larger class of people. In the Summer of 2013, the Obama administration decided to delay by one year the requirement that employers offer health insurance to their employees. Speaker of the House John Boehner reacted by asserting that if big business got relief from the new health care law, it was only fair that families received similar relief from the mandate that individuals obtain health insurance.

We do not expect fairness in all aspects of life: we know that it rains on the just and the unjust alike; bad things do happen to good people; and we regularly tell our children that life is not always fair. Some of us are even as cynical as a character in Cormac McCarthy's *The Crossing*: "He said that while one would like to say that God will punish those who do such things and that people often speak in just that way it was his experience that God could not be spoken for and that men with wicked histories often enjoyed lives of comfort and that they died in peace and were buried with honor. He said that it was a mistake to expect too much justice in this world."[1]

Fairness is, however, an important feature in how we assess the way people treat each other. The claim that someone has acted unfairly is a serious, potentially devastating claim. When we are charged with acting unfairly our response, typically, is not to say "That's right" and then go on about our business. Our response more often is to contest that charge, to defend ourselves. And when it does rain on the just and the unjust, we often provide relief to flood victims. Because people do get cancer, we think about a fair distribution of health care. When we think someone has been treated unjustly, we often initiate a process to provide restitution. In these ways, we act as if fairness is important when we decide how we want our government to act. What fairness means, however, and what it requires is often a contentious matter.

Multiple Criteria

Generalizations about the nature of fairness do not get us very far in making public policy choices, and the movement from general platitudes to more concrete, specific standards is immensely complicated. As a society, we employ many different standards of fairness. A sampling of these includes:

- Equal shares for all: A seemingly simple approach, this is the way we think about voting (one person, one vote), providing elementary school education or fire protection. Everyone in a town gets equal fire protection. A state attempts to provide equal first-grade education to all, unless factors appear which lead us to the next standard.
- To each according to need: In the case of students with disabilities, states often provide more resources for educating those who need more. Food stamps, Medicaid, subsidized housing and college Pell grants are provided to those who need them, and recipients are chosen through some kind of means testing.
- To each according to effort: Unemployment benefits are available to those who worked in jobs, and who lost them for reasons other than their own lack of effort. With the rejection of the something-for-nothing approach, welfare has been transformed into workfare, with provisions that require recipients to work at some point.
- To each based on merit or achievement: Civil service exams are used to sort applicants for government jobs. Admission to colleges comes after a review of an applicant's achievements, and once a student is admitted awards and honors are based on performance.
- To each in recognition of societal contribution: Veterans are awarded extra points on civil service exams because of the service they have rendered to the community. Variations in salaries are often deemed to be fair as indicators of how society values the contributions of different individuals.
- To each according to ability to pay: Mansions and luxury cars are distributed on an ability-to-pay basis, as is much health care (although ability to pay has been viewed as an inappropriate basis for allocating organs for transplantation). The income tax code contains a progressive rate structure that requires high income earners to pay more, because they can.

The list could go on. Age is a factor when certain benefits are provided to children or the elderly. Combat roles, and thus military opportunities, have been restricted by gender. Marital status sometimes makes a difference, as do citizenship and resident status, and perceived needs to compensate for past unfairness. The point is that we, as a society, employ many different, often competing, approaches in determining what is fair or just. Michael Sandel has provided an insightful thumbnail characterization of how the distribution of goods is governed by different standards: "welfare to the needy, honors to the deserving, political power to the persuasive, offices to the qualified, luxuries to those able and willing to pay for them, divine grace to the pious, and so on."[2]

A prominent issue in discussions of fairness is whether the focus should be on opportunity or results. Is it enough that each person has an equal opportunity to compete for benefits, or does fairness require a scheme that will influence the results of that competition? Opponents of affirmative action, for example, argue that equal opportunity should be our goal and that quotas, preferences or other mechanisms that skew outcomes are inherently unfair. Random chance is the distributive mechanism that perfectly insures equal opportunity. And, indeed, sometimes governments and private institutions alike distribute benefits and burdens by random chance. Millions of dollars are distributed through lotteries; many of us remember our selective service numbers being chosen by the luck of the draw; such a mechanism is widely used to allocate seats in magnet schools. We understand tough choices that are made by drawing straws. There is a perception that, when used appropriately, these procedures are fair. Everyone has an equal chance. So, if our *only* goal is equal opportunity, we do have procedures that serve that goal.

Of course, providing for equal opportunity is usually not the only goal that drives the distribution of benefits and burdens in our community. Thus, instead of relying on random assignment we often allocate benefits and burdens, based on factors like past contributions and merit. People are hired who are most likely to do a good job. The students who are admitted to selective educational institutions are those who are most likely to take advantage of the academic program. Salaries are paid that reflect performance and societal valuation of the work.

Therefore, procedures are used that rely on credentials and experience which have not been equally available to all people. To note just one example, parents (with the money to do so) pay expensive tuitions because they are convinced that private schools provided a better opportunity for their children than public schools. The fact is, we do not all start at the same place, and none of us has done anything to deserve our starting place. We are simply born into greater or lesser shares of the features of our lives that shape our success in life's competitions, features such as: mental and physical abilities; family connections and economic resources; certain physical characteristics (such as attractive facial features); social support networks; parents who taught discipline, hard work and delayed gratification; and the like.

Is the use of procedures that rely on academic achievement, credentials and experience fair? The question is especially important when evaluation processes can incorporate cultural or individual biases, and when the results flowing from them lead to outcomes that disproportionately favor certain groups or individuals. For decades, standardized tests have been used for educational admissions decisions; yet, in 2013 an association of 130 private schools in New York ceased to recommend such a test because test-preparation programs and coaching had rendered the test's results meaningless. We want to believe that a fair process will yield fair results, and that we can recognize and design fair processes. We generally consider decisions about allocations to be fair when those decisions are based on factors that are viewed to be relevant, pertinent to the question at hand—as opposed to a perception that political favoritism or economic advantage drives the decision-making process. In reality, it appears that the usefulness of thinking about fairness only in terms of processes, and never results, is limited. In the complex arena of allocating goods and services, observers instinctively sneak a peek at results, or projected results, before being willing to sign on to any process as fair. Agreements on process often break down when participants discover consequences that strike them as unjust.

As we consider what fairness requires in policy making in the pages that follow, it is important to remember that fairness is only one principle that we use to make decisions about allocations. Notions of fairness will often lead us in a different direction than do concerns for benefit and effectiveness. Some decisions are not based on fairness but on something like societal benefit. In one high-profile example, in the aftermath of the 2000 presidential election, Al Gore eventually stopped pursuing legal avenues to contest the outcome. The reason he gave for his decision was not that he thought the Presidency had been fairly awarded to George W. Bush, but that he wanted to avoid the potential harm to the nation that would result from a protracted effort to bring about what he thought would be a just result.

This kind of distinction arises in almost every policy area. A taxation system that focuses only on stimulating economic growth is not going to produce a set of tax rates that many people consider fair. We've had a national debate about whether fairness requires the provision of a minimal level of health care to all U.S. citizens. A different question is whether such health care should be provided as a matter of benefit, either because of the positive contribution to our economy, or because a decent and caring society would want to create that improvement in the well-being of our citizenry. Thus, to say that fairness dictates that a good be distributed in a particular way is different from saying that it should, in fact, be distributed in that way—after other considerations have also been taken into account.

Fairness arguments are not consequential in the same way that arguments from benefit and effectiveness are. Fairness does not ignore the consequences of a policy, because it is interested in whether policies result in fair distributions or assignments of goods and harms, but fairness is less interested in the amount of goods created and harms avoided than it is in the way they are distributed: Are people getting what they deserve? Is their share of the pie just? Are the risks and burdens they are shouldering appropriate? Is compensation for past harms adequate? Does the punishment fit the crime? Such a series of questions implicates a wide and diverse set of moral concerns. Thus, we need to sort out the major elements of these concepts that are found under the broad umbrella of fairness.

Types of Fairness Standards

At its core, fairness requires that people should get what they deserve. In all cases, fairness is about giving people what they are due, but there are multiple grounds upon which to decide what someone is due. As a society, we distribute goods, services and opportunities in a variety of ways. We can group the criteria that have been used into three categories: (1) equal shares, (2) personal behavior, and (3) individual attributes—which often serve as proxies for equal shares and personal behavior.

The first category—an equal distribution that shares certain benefits or opportunities with everyone, regardless of what they might have done to "deserve" them—reflects the view that there are some things that all people deserve. There are some things that people are due, simply because of their status as persons. They would not have to do anything, for example, to earn equal justice under the law, or treatment in an emergency room in a life-threatening situation. Commentators often use the language of "rights" to identify claims of these sorts that persons can make, and the existence of such rights creates duties for others to see that these rights are met.

The equal rights approach holds that fairness requires a distribution of goods that makes people equal in their basic social condition. Sometimes this distribution is understood to require that *primary* goods be provided equally to all people. Primary goods can be understood as the level of basic resources needed to sustain the human pursuit of one's own interests, although the bar can be set at different levels—what is required to survive is different than what is required to thrive. Candidates for inclusion in the grouping of primary goods, in addition to liberty, are food, clothing, shelter, education and basic health care.

Equality plays an important role in our sense of fairness and the implementation of just allocations and distributions. Equal opportunity in employment and education is widely supported. The same is true for the belief that each person's vote should count the same. There are commitments to equal sharing of such public goods as clean air and water, fire department services, and national security. The "equal protection of the laws" is extended to all in the Fourteenth Amendment to our Constitution.

Yet, in many of these areas we do not expect outcomes to be equal. We expect, indeed we have insisted, that different individuals will experience different outcomes in employment, education, and the criminal justice system. These differences are the result of also taking into account the fairness concerns rooted in the second and third categories of personal behavior and individual attributes. The standard of personal behavior, the second category of criteria used for distributive purposes, relates to choices individuals have made: their actions, efforts, achievements and accomplishments. Because of his illegal actions, a criminal fares less well in a court of law than does a law-abiding person. Individuals experience variable success in the employment and education sectors because of their efforts. Some persons are deemed to deserve certain rewards for their achievements; others secure certain benefits because of their willingness to pay for them. We consider these variations in outcome to be fair, as long as the variations are based on the use of relevant criteria.

Applying the standards that justify variable allocations based on actions for which persons are responsible can be a complicated matter. In developing a "bailout" plan in response to the subprime mortgage crisis that arose in 2008 in the United States, some politicians articulated the position that financial assistance should go to those "who need it *and* deserve it." Who deserved such help? Not the "greedy lenders and speculators," who were seen as being responsible for getting themselves into the mess. Many politicians wanted to target low-income homeowners for receipt of this assistance—those who had lost their jobs in the recession (not their fault), who had not understood the terms of their loans (not their fault), who had been misled by lenders (again, not their fault).

The element of personal accountability appears in many policy areas. Some argue that persons who have damaged their livers through excessive use of alcohol should be placed at the bottom of transplant waiting lists for donated livers—if they are allowed on such lists at all. Others view alcoholism as a disease; they attribute less personal accountability for damaging livers through heavy drinking, and thus argue for a place on donated organ lists for alcoholics. Sorting through which types of discriminating distinctions are fair and which are unfair has become more difficult as scientists learn more in their efforts to distinguish between things that are completely within our control and those that may not be.

Recent developments in anti-discrimination law illustrate the tangled web that has been created in attempting to identify the relevance of different factors. For example, providers of health insurance have long been allowed to take predictable risks into account when making decisions about whom to cover and how much to charge for coverage. Such risks were considered to be relevant factors for making business decisions about coverage and rates, although Speaker of the House Nancy Pelosi reflected a changing environment in the summer of 2009 when she accused insurance companies of discriminating against patients because of their pre-existing medical conditions. A difference of opinion has existed about whether it is fair for insurance companies to use a person's medical condition as grounds for denying coverage, or making it prohibitively expensive.

The passage of the Affordable Care Act seems to have settled the issue of denying coverage for now, as even those advocating the abolition of Obamacare voice support for retaining its pre-existing conditions provision—as Mitt Romney did in his 2012 presidential campaign stump speeches.

In the spring of 2008, the Genetic Information Nondiscrimination Act was passed overwhelmingly: unanimously in the Senate, 414–1 in the House (the only negative vote being cast by libertarian Ron Paul), and signed by President Bush. The act prohibits employers and insurance companies from using genetic information to deny employment or insurance coverage or to set premiums based on this information. This act challenges the relevance test that had found health risk to be a legitimate factor in making insurance decisions. This kind of case moves us beyond fairness based on personal choice to the use of individual attributes, the third category of distributive criteria, in making what are considered to be fair allocation decisions.

One attribute that we all share is that we are human beings, and a widely-held belief is that there are certain things—such as life's necessities—that all people deserve because they are human. Attributes that apply to only some persons or groups of persons have also been used in the allocation of goods and burdens, but in two different ways. Some of the individual attributes can be viewed as proxies for the equal shares approach, in terms of trying to level the playing field for opportunity. Other uses of attributes can be viewed as proxies for the personal behavior approach.

As for leveling the opportunity playing field, for centuries, the attributes of race and gender were openly used to discriminate against certain groups of persons in ways that few Americans today would consider fair. More recently, affirmative action plans have used the attributes of race and gender to try to equalize opportunity. Those who believe that prejudice and discrimination still function to unfairly disadvantage members of certain groups are more likely to support affirmative action plans. Those who believe such insidious prejudices are no longer at work in our society are more likely to oppose affirmative action on the grounds that it impedes equal opportunity.

Attributes have been used in other efforts that were undertaken to create equal opportunity when it does not otherwise exist. Accommodations are made for students with learning disabilities in an attempt to give them an opportunity to succeed that is closer to the "normal" baseline. The attribute of age is a basis for programs like Social Security and Medicare, in part out of a perception that the elderly have often lost the ability to compete equally in the marketplace. Benefits are provided to children, who have not yet had an opportunity to provide for themselves. In these and similar cases, policy allocations use attributes to level the playing field.

Individual attributes can also be used as proxies for personal behavior, as markers for one's ability to perform. Aptitude tests are used to allocate jobs and educational opportunities, even though they reflect promises of the potential to achieve rather than achievements themselves. Minors are not allowed to vote, as they are generally viewed as unable to exercise the franchise responsibly. (In centuries past, women were denied the vote for the same reason.) In a different sense, policies that permit the passing down of inherited wealth are a proxy for personal accomplishment, with one individual benefitting from the achievements of others. Those who favor flat tax rates over progressive tax schedules invoke fairness in their argument by saying that the wealthy do not disproportionately benefit from the programs that taxes support, and thus they are unjustly required to pay more.

The use of attributes as the basis of allocations is subject to the test of relevance. Variations in outcomes can be viewed as fair as long as the attributes being used are relevant to the issue at hand. When criteria are employed that are not considered relevant in the particular case (such criteria can include religion, race, gender, age, sexual orientation and national origin), the allocations are judged to be unfair.

The allocation schemes that flow from the two criteria of equal shares and personal behavior (and the attributes related to those two criteria) often pull public policy in different directions. When sorting through this tension, what should we use as our starting point? Should goods, services and opportunities be shared equally, except in cases where there are overriding reasons to allow differential allocations, through the use of attributes or achievements? Or should policy decisions be based on behavior and achievements which yield disparate outcomes, until the resulting inequality offends our sense of fairness? Different answers to these questions grow out of differing fundamental views about the proper role of government.

Many of the disagreements about the meaning of fairness break down along two different starting points or baselines, two different inclinations about the role government should play in our community's life. One starting point has been called the watchdog state or the night watchman state, a view that the government's fundamental role is to protect us from one another. The emphasis here is on freedom, and on the rights to "life, liberty and the pursuit of happiness" identified in the Declaration of Independence. The other starting point is the welfare state, which emphasizes justice, equality, and the concern to "promote the general welfare" that is identified in the U.S. Constitution. The first focuses on a conception of liberty that is "freedom from" obstacles that interfere with the pursuit of our own interests. The latter focuses on a conception of liberty that entails a concern for the resources required to give citizens the "freedom to" pursue those interests. The way in which the language of fairness and justice has permeated advocacy of both approaches calls for a review of these two alternative philosophies.

The Liberty Baseline

This first approach to the government's role in matters of fairness and justice begins with liberty. Robert Nozick provides a classic statement of this position on individual liberty and rights. He concludes that "a minimal state, limited to the narrow functions of protection against force, theft, fraud, enforcement of contracts, and so on, is justified; that any more extensive state will violate persons' rights not to be forced to do certain things, and is unjustified."[3]

The libertarian position is that each person has a fundamental right to liberty—to do whatever he or she wants, as long as the rights of others to do the same are not violated. The only role for the state is to protect this right: to provide security, punish theft and fraud, protect property, enforce contracts, and so forth. Each of us has a right to decide what to do with our bodies, our labor and our goods. Government policies that interfere with this right distribute resources in ways that are unfair. In the words of James Madison, a just government is one "which impartially secures to every man whatever is his own."

The story that works for those who accept this approach is the one told by Thomas Hobbes in *Leviathan* in 1660. In a state of nature, life for humans is "solitary, poor, nasty, brutish and short." They thus act to form governments to protect themselves, through a very limited contract which allows maximum individual liberty and authorizes government action only to the extent that that action provides personal security, in order to make life a little less brutish and a little less short. Modern day appropriations of this story emphasize the maintenance of individual liberty and spheres of autonomy. One implication of this approach is clear on the issue of taxation. "Taxation of earnings from labor," wrote Nozick, "is on par with forced labor."[4] If the purpose of government is to preserve a sizeable zone of autonomy for individuals, a fair tax system is one that preserves what an individual has. What do people deserve? They deserve to keep what they have. The only basis for any re-distribution of current holdings is the rectification of injustice. Libertarians believe that we deserve what we have acquired—as long as those possessions were not acquired by force or fraud.

Nozick does recognize limitations on property rights, limitations based on a principle articulated by John Locke that the distribution of property must leave enough in common for others to ensure that one person's acquisition does not worsen the situation of others. But Nozick's view of such worsening seems to apply only to avoiding catastrophe—for example, one should not own the only oasis in a desert and charge prohibitive fees for water. This limit is mostly discussed by Nozick in terms of the monopolization of necessities. His final judgment is that the free operation of a market system will not actually run afoul of the Lockean proviso, and thus this limit on acquisition will not in reality provide significant opportunities for state action.

The Liberty Baseline begins with the default position of no government intervention. The presumption is that individuals should be left to run their own lives. Absent such a rationale as restitution for past injustices, government policies that allocate goods and services are unfair. This presumption is based in the imagined natural state in which each person retained complete autonomy over his or her life. Only when these individuals voluntarily entered into a contract, voluntarily surrendering their autonomy in exchange for security of person and possessions, did it become legitimate for others, through societal governing institutions, to impinge on their liberty in any way. And the only fair ways to interfere with the exercise of liberty are those that protect and enhance one's autonomy.

The Welfare Baseline

From another point of view, fairness is important because we care about people's well-being. Fairness has bite because we are allocating limited resources. If we could give all people everything they wanted, then allocation decisions would not attract so much attention. The reality is, of course, that we can't meet all needs, and certainly not all desires, so we are left with distributional schemes that result in some people getting less of some things that they want, and in some cases less than they need. We are inevitably involved in the rationing of resources. Fairness is especially important when addressing access to the goods and services required to engage in life's basic activities. For many, government should play a role not only in providing for the common welfare, but also in seeing that the commonwealth extends fairly to all citizens.

We saw that advocates of the Liberty Baseline begin with a state-of-nature story, but critics of that approach counter that this story imagines a state of nature that has never existed, and which never could have existed. In the Welfare Baseline counter-story, the true state of nature is community. The human race, and each member of it, has come into being in community, as a community. The natural default position is not one of autonomous individuals, free from interference by others, but of inter-dependent members of a group who rely on others and upon whom others rely. Human life was never solitary. This reality provides support for a starting point for a distributive process in which communal structures allocate goods and services equitably.

While libertarians focus on process and opportunity, welfarists incorporate an interest in outcomes and results in their assessments. They do not see their task as designing a process for the distribution of goods and services and then turning a blind eye to the allocation of benefits that the process yields. In fact, a process that might appear to be fair can be judged otherwise when the results are in. A process can be judged by its results—by whether people get what they are due, what they deserve. A process that might meet theoretical tests for fairness in the abstract could be found to be unjust when its use in a real-world context brings about inequitable consequences.

The interest in welfare supports a role for government that is more than serving only as a referee to prevent the most egregious infractions of theft and violence. This more expansive role includes responsibilities to see that basic needs are met, that the goods that are required for human flourishing are available to all. Whereas the focus on liberty makes an effort to restore a world of free actions by unfettered, autonomous individuals, the focus on welfare makes an effort to replicate the largely informal and personal inter-actions of small group settings, in camps and clans and villages and tribes—in an imagined time when the group looked out for the welfare of each of its members.

The problem for both approaches is one of scale. The pursuit of fairness in modern society requires massive formal mechanisms. We have so many people, who are so interconnected, living in so little space, that questions about government regulation are no longer questions of "if" but "how" and "how much." The Great Recession of the early twenty-first century, in which so many suffered unfairly because of the deeds of others, is only the most recent demonstration of the necessity of governmental oversight. If public policies will inevitably play a role in our community's welfare, the question is how that role can be fulfilled responsibly and fairly.

In the delivery of health care services, a welfare-based approach to fairness is interested in medical care being provided to all on an equitable basis. Such a system would be designed to allocate services to those who need them, perhaps within the constraints of cost-effectiveness guidelines. A single-payer system would be the most straightforward method of providing this care. Many object to such a plan, arguing that health care would be rationed, in violation of the liberty principle. Of course, health care is also rationed in a system designed to implement the liberty baseline, only in this latter case it is often rationed according to one's ability to pay for the services.

The current health care system in the U.S. is a mixture of liberty and welfare concerns reflecting our nation's commitments to both sets of values. Any feasible alternative to present-day health care policy will continue to embody elements of this hybrid approach. A plan that provides basic health care to all will still, inevitably, allow for a second tier of services (elective, experimental, less cost-effective, or highly-priced services) for those who can pay for them. And, as a practical matter, any plan that emphasizes liberty will still contain elements based on the welfare approach (such as Medicare, Medicaid, preventive care for children, life-saving emergency room care, or waiting lists for transplantable organs).

Some argue that policies that allow for different levels of health care are inherently unjust. But the only way to avoid differential levels would be to adopt policies that either (1) provide everyone with all the treatment they want, irrespective of what they could pay for, or (2) refuse to allow individuals to pay for treatments beyond the level of care that could be guaranteed for all. Not only are both of these alternatives impractical, it is difficult to see how a case could be made that fairness requires either of these options.

The Welfare Baseline and the Liberty Baseline provide a stark contrast in theoretical beginning points for deciding what fairness requires in our policy making. If we grant, as I do, that there is value in both approaches, then the question is how to incorporate both sets of concerns in our assessment of public policies. More specifically, should one of these approaches be given priority over the other?

Choosing a Baseline?

The divide in our country between the autonomous individual story and the interdependent community story was grandly displayed at the 2012 Republican National Convention in Tampa. Earlier that summer, President Obama highlighted a piece of the interdependent community story, saying:

> If you were successful, somebody along the line gave you some help. There was a great teacher somewhere in your life. Somebody helped to create this unbelievable American system that we have that allowed you to thrive. Somebody invested in roads and bridges. If you've got a business—you didn't build that.

The Republican Party's response was to counter with the autonomous individual story. "We Built It" was the theme of the second night of the convention, with nearly every speaker making some reference to the President's remark. Most speakers told their own personal stories of achieving and "building" as well as those of their constituents and friends, and the crowd chanted "We Built It" through much of the evening. The Obama story was one of community and government enhancing societal welfare, the Republican story was one of personal achievement that is possible when individuals are free to work and innovate.

Should we evaluate the fairness of policies by beginning with a certain primacy established for liberty or for social welfare? One option would be to start with the liberty baseline and then move off of it for good reasons, including reasons based in concerns for the well-being of the community. Another option would be to start with the welfare baseline and then move off of it for good reasons, including reasons based in concerns for liberty. I believe that neither approach is advisable.

John Rawls, in his presentation of justice as fairness, offered the most widely-known effort to combine these competing concepts of fairness. He thought that the problem with reaching agreement about what constitutes fairness is that all persons' views are influenced by their own interests. Each person knows how one approach to justice or another would affect her own outcome, and this knowledge biases conclusions about what fairness requires. Rawls proposed a mental experiment in which individuals assume an original position—a position in which they have no knowledge of their own natural endowments or abilities, their economic or social place in society, their race or gender or religion. Behind such a veil of ignorance, he said, individuals making choices about principles of justice would not choose unfair standards, because they would know that they could end up on the losing end of the application of such unjust standards.

The fundamental outcome of this mental experiment was enunciated by Rawls as follows: "The general conception of justice as fairness requires that all primary social goods be distributed equally unless an unequal distribution would be to everyone's advantage."[5] By primary goods, he means the "things that every rational man is presumed to want." More specifically, he believed that deliberation from the original position would lead to the selection of two principles: (1) equal liberty and equality of opportunity for all persons; and (2) acceptance of social inequalities as fair, only if they maximize, or at least contribute to, the long-term expectations of the least fortunate group in society.[6] He explicitly mentions the possibility of accepting inequalities that would set up incentives to encourage more productive efforts in society as a whole. So a fair economic system could be one that allows for an unequal distribution of wealth, to the extent that that inequality is produced by incentives that lead to outcomes that also result in everyone being better off.

There are good reasons to begin our reasoning about policies with the welfare baseline. First, we become individuals in community. Therefore, theoretically, community is prior. It makes sense to begin with a model of an interdependent community, with each of us being responsible for one another's welfare. Second, we do not "deserve" our innate advantages. None of us deserve the intelligence or physical attributes we were born with, our family connections, inherited wealth, or the country we happen to be born in. And we do little, if anything, to deserve the value that others place on such attributes.

Inevitably, societies are structured in ways that privilege some attributes over others. Advocates of a liberty baseline would tend to agree that individuals like Warren Buffett and Bill Gates deserve what they have earned through their success in the modern marketplace. My suspicion is that individuals with the same abilities that have enabled Buffett and Gates to be successful would have fared less well if they were born centuries ago into cultures that valued prowess in combat more highly than business acumen. The point is that to a considerable extent those among us who have been successful have been fortunate to find themselves in a context that values their abilities—a good fortune that they themselves did not earn. Some of us have benefited more than others from the particular social structures that govern all of our lives.

Third, liberty does not make any sense as a concept without a basic level of resources. A person can exercise his autonomy only if he possesses at least minimal resources. Making use of one's liberty does not require equal resources, but the allocation of a certain level of goods is a necessary prerequisite for liberty to flourish. In a more pragmatic vein, if we need to include both the interests of liberty and the interests of welfare in the making of just public policy, we can ask: from which baseline is the journey to the middle more difficult in the real world? The answer almost certainly is that beginning with the liberty baseline presents a more obstacle-filled path for those who want to move final judgments toward some kind of balance. Consider the two starting points: if we begin with the presumption of liberty, we would then add balance by overriding autonomy by "spreading the wealth around." The powerful and well-to-do will have plenty of clout to protect their positions—to prevent too-large an imbalance in the distribution of resources from undermining their autonomy and liberty. The disadvantaged with fewer resources will have a more difficult time overriding a presumption in favor of liberty in their effort to reach an equitable allocation of goods and services. If, on the other hand, we begin with the presumption of the welfare of individuals, we would then add balance by acknowledging the importance of respecting personal liberty and the critical role that individual freedom plays in enhancing total community welfare. The abundant resources of the "haves" would facilitate this movement to a policy middle.

In the end, however, a presumption in favor of either of these baselines does not contribute constructively to assessments of policies in terms of fairness. Such a presumption is not helpful, because there are too many exceptions, too many of the "other reasons," reasons rooted in the different yet valid conceptions of fairness itself. Any one-size-fits-all theory, such as Rawls's, will be too general to be of much use, will leave out important valid considerations, or both. Judgments about fair policies should emerge from specific policy discussions, within the context of unique sets of circumstances. The following section suggests ways to find fairness in specific contexts in the absence of grand conceptual schemes that privilege either liberty or welfare.

Fairness in Different Contexts

Community Failure

We have noted how government acts in the pursuit of effectiveness when market failures interfere with the efficient allocation of economic resources. In an analogous way, government acts in the pursuit of fairness when community failures create environments that fall short of the demands of justice. In the same way that economists have analyzed and understood market failures, and determined when government intervention is appropriate to correct for those failures, we should analyze and understand community failures and determine how government should make policy in response to the demands of fairness. The market, when it functions properly, maximizes effectiveness and benefit. Our social institutions, when they function properly, should promote fair treatment for all.

When you find a law that prohibits an action, there is a good chance that someone was engaging in that action. When you find a law that requires certain actions, there is a good chance that individuals have been failing to act in that way. It is easy to identify current government policies and regulations that were unheard of in the past. These policies are not required to govern, but rather have appeared in light of findings that our community was failing to meet obligations of fairness. In some cases, the understanding of the meaning of fairness changed. In other cases, the less formal, communal governing practices of simpler times ceased to function adequately.

For example, we have anti-discrimination legislation because, in the judgment of many, the community failed to establish a just environment for those seeking jobs and education. We have Social Security, and Medicare and food stamp programs because of judgments that the community failed to provide adequate resources for many in our society. We have laws requiring accommodations for the disabled because of the community's failure to provide appropriate accommodations. In the aftermath of the Great Recession, we saw efforts to pass more extensive financial regulations because the community failed to operate a financial system that was fair to all segments of our population.

Most of us share the aspiration that the fair treatment of all people should be the hallmark of interactions among individuals in our society. The hope is that people acting in good faith—along with such non-governmental institutions as businesses, churches, families and civic organizations—will set a tone and enforce just and fair interactions throughout the community. Sometimes these efforts fail. Just as we can identify causes for market failure (negative externalities, monopolies, information asymmetries), so we can identify causes for community failure: self-interest, prejudice, inadequate information, fear, inertia that favors the status quo. The community has failed when, in the compassionate conservative campaign rhetoric of George W. Bush, anyone is "left behind." We also want to avoid a governmental role which contributes to community failure, which can happen when an active government crowds out its rivals, those private communal organizations through which we can also work collectively in the pursuit of the common good.

Elements of Fairness Assessments

How should we decide which understanding of fairness should apply in given cases? How should we assess the fairness of a policy that provides Medicare to all citizens, regardless of their income level? Or a proposal that a public high school education should be provided only to children whose intellectual abilities rank them in the top half of their cohort? Or that would extend voting rights only to property owners? What does "equitable" or "desert" mean in these and other imaginable scenarios?

Three key ingredients in such assessments of fairness are: (1) what is being distributed; (2) to whom is it being distributed; and (3) the basis on which the distribution should be made. The "what" that is being allocated includes benefits, goods, services, opportunities, and rewards. This aspect of fair treatment also includes the negative side of the ledger: the allocation of harms, costs, burdens, risks, and punishments. The "whom" that will be on the receiving end of the treatment can include all persons affected by a government's action, or more limited groups: only citizens, residents, legal residents, or some subset of these groups. A debate continues about the inclusion of non-human subjects in the fashioning of fair policies.[7]

The heart of fairness assessments is usually the "how," the way in which allocations take place. These determinations, however, are largely a function of the particular things being allocated and the persons who are subject to the allocation decisions. Applications of the fairness principle have and will vary from situation to situation, depending on the parties involved and the subjects being addressed. Ethically, this case-sensitive approach is more appropriate than a blanket imposition of one fairness scheme in all times and in all places.

The identification of the things that are being allocated is an important step in the assessment process. Disputes about the requirements of fairness are often generated by a lack of precision at this point. Disagreements rage about how "health care" should be distributed fairly, often with little attention being paid to the great variety that exists among types of health care. For example, one's view about the appropriateness of using a willingness-to-pay standard could be different for life-saving treatment in emergency rooms and for elective cosmetic surgery. One could make finer distinctions between the cosmetic surgeries that restore one's appearance after treatment for cancer and surgeries that enhance one's appearance by giving them features they never had. The prospect of using variable standards for establishing just allocations expands further when health care not only includes a smallpox vaccination and setting a broken bone, but also includes herbal remedies, wellness programs, yoga, meditation, and aerobic and strength exercise programs.

Attention to detail is also important when assessing the ways in which the distributive processes would work. A national debate about affirmative action is in its sixth decade in the United States, but advocates on both sides of the issue often stake out their claims without offering any clear statements about what "affirmative action" means. The argument is about a label, rather than about the ways in which particular allocation processes would operate. If one believes that race or gender can be an appropriate consideration in the fair allocation of employment opportunities, acting affirmatively can mean many different things, such as: (1) advertising positions in a way that increases the probability that women and persons of color would know about vacant positions; (2) engaging in public relations activities that would likely encourage women and minority candidates to apply; (3) holding searches open for a longer period of time in an effort to achieve a representative pool of applicants; (4) setting goals that would serve as aspirational targets in an effort to increase diversity; (5) taking race and gender into account, among other factors, when choosing among qualified applicants;

(6) adopting rigid quotas that would guarantee that the workforce became representative. Constructive conversations about the pros and cons of such more-defined courses of action such as these six should replace broadsides that affirm or deny the fairness of all of the possibilities that could be swept up under the generality of "affirmative action."

We can add the element of "why" to the "what," the "who," and the "how" of the allocation of benefits and harms. The assignment and division of goods, services and opportunities is done for a purpose, and it is appropriate to fashion distribution policies that reflect the purposes we are attempting to serve. On this score, the distinction between primary goods and other goods makes a difference. Primary goods are those things that are necessary to pursue our life plans, which are required in order for a person to act on opportunities. These are goods whose lack will cause pain and suffering and derail an individual's best efforts to succeed. It is with this purpose in mind that we think about the provision of food and health care. Other non-essential goods and services do not have the same effect on basic well-being and equality of opportunity, and thus we have different purposes in mind when assessing allocation arrangements for golf club memberships, Porsches, and diamond jewelry.

Purpose has implications for fairness in other arenas of our lives. We allocate the right to vote for one purpose. We mete out punishment in the criminal justice system, we protect private property, and we admit students to highly-subsidized Ph.D. programs in physics all for different purposes. Still other purposes are served in the allocation of tax burdens—what is fair will differ depending on whether the purpose is to preserve individual autonomy or promote the welfare of the larger community. Fair decisions are those based on relevant factors, and the purposes to be served help us identify the factors that are relevant in particular cases. These factors, these considerations provide the base points for deciding what people are due, what they deserve, what it means to treat them equitably. As a beginning point, what every person is due, what every person deserves, is that we give careful thought and collective deliberation to what constitutes fair and just treatment. Fairness will occupy its rightful place in policy evaluation only as we are willing for the conclusions of this deliberation to modify the policy outcomes that flow from calculations of benefit and effectiveness. And justice will most likely be done when the context-specific assessments constitute a clear-eyed navigation of the issues with a focus not on ideological rigidity but on the persons whose welfare and lives are weighed in the balance.

Notes

1 Cormac McCarthy, *The Crossing* (New York: Alfred A. Knopf, 1994), p. 288.
2 Michael J. Sandel, *Public Philosophy: Essays on Morality in Politics* (Cambridge, MA: Harvard University Press, 2005), p. 175.

3 Robert Nozick, *Anarchy, State, and Utopia* (New York: Basic Books, 1974), p. ix.
4 Ibid., p. 169.
5 Rawls, *A Theory of Justice*, p. 150.
6 Ibid., p. 151.
7 This discussion of justice and fairness has been limited to persons. An important issue, which is dealt with only in passing in this book, is the extent to which non-human species should be included in such discussions. Sometimes the standing of animals to have their welfare considered is couched in terms of "animal rights," that these are beings with an interest in avoiding pain and untimely death and the purpose of rights is to protect such interests.

For Tom Regan, animals are "subjects-of-a-life," like human beings, and as such have inherent worth that entitles them to live their lives with respect and autonomy. Within this frame of reference, promoting human benefit cannot excuse violating these rights: "The laudatory achievements of science, including the many genuine benefits obtained for both humans and animals, do not justify the unjust means used to secure them. . . . Such research should go on—but not at the expense of laboratory animals." *The Case for Animal Rights* (London: Routledge, 1984), p. 397.

6   Honoring Commitments
Fidelity

We want governments to act faithfully in their dealings with those who are governed. In the broadest sweep, fidelity reflects our desire that governance be respectful of persons. The belief that persons should be treated as ends, and not merely as instrumentalities, points us to distinctive governmental obligations in addition to those that are grounded in the other benchmarks. Some of these fidelity obligations flow from promises and explicit commitments governments have made. Others flow from the nature of governance itself, or from specific forms of governance such as a democratic republic. Some commentators have identified other presumed obligations that are implied in particular interactions between those who govern and the governed, and yet other duties have been identified that are assumed from external sources. A moral analysis of public policy should include an assessment of how faithful a government is in meeting these kinds of obligations.

At the 1993 Fourth of July celebration in Dubuque, Iowa, Senator Charles Grassley stood on the back of a flatbed trailer overlooking the banks of the Mississippi River and spoke to the audience of a promise made by the U.S. Government. Grassley repeatedly spoke the words of the promise: "Thou shalt not be forgotten." The color guard in the Independence Day ceremony paraded the promise by the crowd on a black POW/MIA flag as the state's senior senator reminded the onlookers of a national commitment.

"Thou shalt not be forgotten." This is a promise, Grassley said, that is made to all persons who join the Armed Services: if war comes, and you are captured, you will not be forgotten. At that time, the importance of that promise for the Senator lay in the fact that discussions were under way about the normalization of relations between the United States and Vietnam. In the most significant step toward normalization since the end of the Vietnam War in 1975, President Bill Clinton had just announced the United States would no longer oppose international loans to Vietnam. Acting alone, the United States had previously blocked offers by France and Japan to pay $140 million of Hanoi's debts to the International Monetary Fund. Payment of that debt would have allowed the IMF to make new loans to Vietnam.

President Clinton had chosen a two-pronged approach: permitting international loans to Vietnam while at the same time sending a high-level delegation to Hanoi to press for more information about American soldiers who were still Missing-in-Action from the war. Clinton hoped that such a policy would yield more progress in the accounting for missing veterans. "To encourage further progress," he stated, "it is appropriate at this time to recognize what the Vietnamese have done in our effort to account for the missing."

At that time, more than 2,200 Americans were still listed as missing in action in Southeast Asia, 1,650 of them in Vietnam itself. Should the United States normalize relations with Vietnam? Should the United States permit international loans to Vietnam and clear the way for new IMF loans? For Grassley the answer was clear. The country should keep its promise and refuse to cooperate with or provide assistance to that country—even if doing so would be "good for business." Grassley feared that the forces pushing for a change in U.S. policy were more interested in economic benefits than in accounting for the missing soldiers. Promises should not be forgotten, he argued, even if substantial benefits would result.

The Senator believed that developing U.S. policy toward Vietnam should not be based only on calculations of benefit and effectiveness, but should include commitments embodied in the concept of fidelity. The key to understanding fidelity is relationship. What one person owes another is partially determined by the ways in which the one person is related to the other. Relationships that are commonly cited in this regard are the relations between parents and children, other family members, friends, members of a cultural community, and citizens of the same state or nation. Relationships are also established through contracts, promises, covenants and other actions that cause individuals to believe that they can rely on others in certain ways.

The relationship that grounds the norm of fidelity in the assessment of policy is the relationship that exists between a government (local, state or national) and its citizens. Since "the government" should be an agent that acts of behalf of its citizens, the relationship that grounds fidelity can be understood more deeply as the relationship which exists among the members of a community, as that relationship is mediated through governmental institutions and representatives. To some extent, fidelity interests also extend to other residents, and even non-residents who have reasons to rely on a government to act in certain ways. The transnational aspect of the responsibilities of fidelity was on display in March of 2009 when Chinese premier Wen Jiabao expressed concerns about U.S. debt levels, warning America to "honor its word" and ensure the safety of Chinese assets.

A fundamental moral basis for the benchmark of fidelity is the notion of respect for human dignity that is expressed in Immanuel Kant's imperative that people be treated as ends and not merely as means to ends. The belief that persons should not be treated only as instrumentalities places limits on how government should relate to individuals, and to the citizenry as a whole. The principle of fidelity is concerned with faithfulness to the demands of respect and dignity. The basic idea is that a government has obligations that should be honored, even if keeping a promise or fulfilling a commitment may not produce the most beneficial or effective outcome in a particular case. Senator Grassley's position on the Vietnam issue supplies an example of how a beneficial economic policy can conflict with perceived obligations of fidelity. The pull of fidelity can also be seen in the practice of "grandfathering," when policy changes are desirable for reasons of benefit or effectiveness but the people who are "owed" under past agreements are spared the impact of the desired changes.

The discussion of fidelity that follows organizes into four categories the grounds for expectations that citizens and others have of government: (1) specific commitments that have been made; (2) structural requirements embedded in the institutions of governance; (3) implied or presumed obligations; and (4) obligations that have been assumed from external sources.

Commitments Made

One type of obligation consists of responsibilities that a government has acquired by its own specific actions. These types of commitments include such things as contracts with private corporations, pension obligations established for government workers, and setting deadlines for the achievement of certain policy objectives. The expectation is established that the government will be faithful in its dealings—honoring contracts, keeping promises, adhering to self-imposed limitations. In this category of cases, there have been concrete declarations of governmental obligation.

Examples of such commitments range across all areas of government. State agencies have told parents that records will remain confidential and their identities will be kept secret if they place their children for adoption with those agencies—but after the fact those policies have been changing. Explicit commitments made by government most often attract notice when the commitments are not fulfilled. In the summer of 2012, the city of Scranton, Pennsylvania, slashed the pay of every city employee to $7.25 an hour—the minimum wage—in violation of the rates of pay contained in union contracts with the city. A statutory deadline of January 9, 2008, had been established for reaching a decision on the fate of the polar bear under the Endangered Species Act. The U.S. Fish and Wildlife Service missed that deadline, adopted a new self-imposed deadline of 30 additional days, and then missed that one. The Environmental Protection Agency promised to rule on whether coal ash should be classified as a hazardous material by the end of 2009, but failed to do so. In these types of cases, conflicts arise when there appears to be a failure to fulfill the commitments that have been made.

In retrospect, it may become clear that a promise was a mistake. For reasons of effectiveness or fairness, the after-the-fact judgment could be that the promise should never have been made. Abandoning such a promise is possible, but the process of revoking such a commitment should be a complicated one, taking into account such factors as reliance on the promise that some people have developed in their own actions, giving notice of the change, and the possibilities for mitigating the impact of the change on those who will be adversely affected. We are not forever and absolutely bound to mistaken promises. We do have an obligation to take care in how we renege on our obligations.

A fundamental way in which many governments have made commitments to "the people," or that the people have made commitments to one another through governing bodies, is through the adoption of constitutions. Such documents represent not only a compact among a particular group at a particular time, but ways in which one generation binds future generations. The obligations that follow from this kind of commitment can be both procedural (presidents will be chosen by electoral votes, not popular votes) and substantive (citizens will not be treated in cruel and inhumane ways).

Constitutions occupy a peculiar place in our legal systems. The idea in Western political thought that a higher law should operate to constrain governments and to judge rulers reaches back to Biblical-era Judaism. Since the Middle Ages, political thinkers have conceived of law in two forms: ordinary law promulgated by governing rulers, and higher law that arises from sources beyond the government's boundaries and binds rulers as well as subjects. The basis for this higher law has been identified in such various sources as natural law, divine law, or the people. In modern times, higher law has been codified into definitive form in foundational documents such as constitutions. These documents mediate these at times vaguely-defined notions of higher law in a way that channels debate about their meaning into reasonably manageable social discourse. When such codification occurs, a society is making explicit commitments, establishing new specific obligations that incorporate these previously extra-legal standards. The community adopts a set of principles by which the government will be (or at least should be) constrained. The aspects of "higher law" which are codified in this way become explicit commitments which fall within this first type of fidelity obligations.

Structural Requirements

The demands of fidelity also apply to obligations that are built into the structure of governing. Government is accountable not only for particular explicit commitments but also for doing business in an appropriate way. The very structure of making and enforcing laws and regulations must meet certain requirements if government is to be faithful to the governed. Lon Fuller's book *The Morality of Law* presents a classic description of this understanding of obligation.[1] His description of the "internal morality of law" identifies a set of criteria that he believed any legal regime must satisfy in order for its governing actions to be expressions of authority rather than uses of pure force. He identified eight demands of the law's inner morality, and concluded that a total failure in any one of the eight areas results in something that is not properly called a legal system at all. A brief summary of these eight requirements provides a concrete illustration of this aspect of fidelity.

First, there must be rules—general rules, standards that apply to all, so that every issue is not decided on an ad hoc or personal basis. Second, legal rules must be promulgated. They must be published and publicly known. The story of Caligula's inaccessible laws that were posted at the top of columns in small print so they could not be read provides a counter-example to this requirement. Third, laws should speak prospectively, not retroactively. Law has to do with the governance of human conduct by rules, but in Fuller's words, "To speak of governing or directing conduct today by rules that will be enacted tomorrow is to talk in blank prose."[2]

Fuller's fourth and fifth stipulations are that laws be clear, and that they not be contradictory. Obscure, incoherent and undecipherable policies and laws, and also those that are self-contradictory or in irreconcilable conflict with others, are functionally no governance at all. The same can be said for laws that require the impossible, which is Fuller's sixth requirement, and for laws that change so frequently that subjects cannot orient their action in accordance with them—which violates Fuller's seventh requirement that laws be constant over time.

Fuller considered his final standard, congruence between official action and declared rule, to be the most complex. In this eighth requirement, he is interested in consistency between the rules as they are announced and the rules as they are actually administered. He notes that this congruence may be destroyed or impaired in a variety of ways: "mistaken interpretation, inaccessibility of the law, lack of insight into what is required to maintain the integrity of a legal system, bribery, prejudice, indifference, stupidity, and the drive toward personal power."[3] The fundamental point is that there must be, for any government worth the name, a consistency between law as it is stated and proclaimed, and law as it is actually practiced and enforced.

This insistence on congruence between law as stated and as actually enforced admits to degrees of deviance. Examples abound. The failure to enforce, until its repeal in 2005, a 1675 Massachusetts law that ordered the arrest of American Indians who entered the city of Boston, was not considered a fatal flaw of congruence for that state's legal regime. For many observers, President Franklin Roosevelt's agreement with British Prime Minister Winston Churchill to send 50 U.S. destroyers to Great Britain in exchange for the right to use nine British military bases in the run up to World War II, in arguable violation of statutory law, would fall into a category of justified exceptions to this requirement of fidelity. On the other hand, divided opinions about the Iran-Contra affair, in which arms were sold in exchange for the release of U.S hostages in a secret deal (with the funds funneled to Nicaraguan rebels in circumvention of existing legislation), illustrate the more troublesome complications that can arise when exceptions to Fuller's basic principles are accepted.

Degrees of deviance and possible justifications of exceptions apply to all of the elements of Fuller's inner morality of law. The effective pursuit of national security interests often leads to deviations from the requirement that policies and regulations should be made public, such as the Transportation Security Agency's insistence on keeping secret its regulations governing the screening of passengers in airports. Tax laws that are believed to be necessary for the effective management of a nation's economy or a government's budget often have had a retroactive effect. The norm that laws remain constant over time quickly gives way to the norm of effectiveness when it is discovered that a regulation results in unintended consequences or when circumstances change dramatically.

The structural requirements described by Fuller introduce us to a kind of reciprocal fidelity. His inner morality of law is a description of the kind of legal regime that deserves the fidelity of its citizens. It describes a legal regime that has been faithful in its obligations to the citizenry, and thus warrants the loyalty and obedience of those who are governed. Fuller developed his thinking about the inner morality of law in the context of a debate about the validity of actions during the Third Reich, actions that had been carried out in accordance with the established law at the time. The question being debated was whether the reallocations of property and the deprivations of liberty that resulted from the reprehensible policies of the Nazi regime should be honored after the fall of that government. Some commentators argued that those policies should not be honored, and that retroactive laws should be passed that would invalidate the laws and policies of the Third Reich—thus nullifying the results that flowed from those flawed statutes and policies. Fuller agreed that these reallocations and deprivations should not be honored, but his solution to the problem was to declare that the Nazi regime was no valid regime at all. The governance of Germany during this time so completely failed the tests of law's inner morality for him that those policies were without force and were undeserving of obedience, thus providing no cover for those who had acted pursuant to those laws. Similar issues were raised after the fall of the Berlin wall, when guards who had been stationed on that wall were arrested and charged for following orders and shooting civilians who were fleeing East Germany.

The tradition of civil disobedience grew out of this understanding of mutual fidelity. Citizens owe allegiance and obedience to regimes which deserve their faithfulness. When a government fails to adopt policies and pass laws that meet its obligations to the citizenry, reciprocity can hardly be expected or warranted. This was the case in such instances as the violation of segregation ordinances that sparked the Civil Rights movement in the United States, and the non-violent resistance led by Mahatma Gandhi that resulted in independence for India. The reverse is also true: when a regime is faithful, when it acts in accordance with its obligations to the governed, then responsibility is established for the people to support and defend that regime. Sometimes this reciprocal fidelity can be expressed in an action as simple as voting in an election, when the act of casting a vote is motivated by a sense of civic duty or responsibility. This is not blind loyalty, but loyalty given in a mutual exchange as the relationship between the governed and those who govern is strengthened in the pursuit of a common vision of the good society.

Fuller's internal morality of law speaks to the structural requirements of any governing regime. It applies to *all* governments, regardless of form. However, additional obligations of fidelity also flow from particular types and forms of governments. Consider, for example, a republic. By its very nature a republican form of government is limited government and those limitations impose obligations upon the governors to the citizens. The precise ways in which republican government is limited have been a matter of ongoing debate among historians, political scientists and legal scholars.[4] Republics in general, and that of the United States in particular, are not dictatorships or totalitarian regimes. The limits that distinguish the republican form from other types of governments are themselves features of structural fidelity obligations.

Structural obligations also arise from other particular types of government. As a point of comparison with secular republics, we can note parallel limitations on those who govern in states that are organized with elements of a theocracy. In a theocracy, religious law is embedded in the governing institutions and processes. In the same way that the acts of policy makers in a republic should be constrained by the limitations inherent in that form of government, the acts of policy makers in a theocracy should be constrained by religious dictates. (We can voice our objections to theocratic forms of government and still recognize the internal obligations imposed on the leaders in those systems.) Modern day examples include those nations in which Sharia, the Islamic law that governs all aspects of life, is structurally embedded in the government. In Iran, ultimate authority rests with two offices reserved for Shia clerics—the Supreme Leader of Iran and the Guardian Council. Saudi Arabia is a monarchy in which the Quran has constitutional status and whose legislation is a codified version of Sharia. In the countries whose governments claim to implement Sharia, whose legitimacy rests on its adherence to that Islamic law, a structural requirement of fidelity is that laws and policies conform to that religious tradition.

Presumed Obligations

We also hear commentators and citizens speak of the need for those who govern to be faithful to a third type of obligation. These commitments are neither inherent in the structure of the government nor explicitly spelled out in prior government action. Rather, they are inferred from past understandings and interactions between the government and the people whose lives it affects. Senator Grassley's "Thou shalt not be forgotten" reflects his view of an implied obligation. The same could be said of Secretary of Defense William Cohen's conclusion in 1998: "I have concluded that we must honor our commitment to attempt to locate and identify the remains of all Americans lost in combat." The issue Cohen was addressing was whether the tomb of America's Unknown Soldier from the Vietnam War should be opened in an attempt to determine the identity of the remains. A Pentagon spokesperson echoed Cohen's statement, saying that the government had an "obligation" to the family of one missing soldier, and that "We also have an obligation to all of those who have served in wars in the past and who view this site as very hallowed ground."

Examples of this sort are often found in the military context and arose repeatedly as the United States prosecuted the war in Iraq. In the spring of 2009, Secretary of Defense Robert Gates stated that the practice of holding troops past the end of their enlistment commitments (the "stop-loss" program) was "breaking faith" with those soldiers. These same notions of commitment and obligation appear in discussions of the medical care being provided by the Veterans Administration to veterans of the Iraq and Afghan wars. In a more general sense, fidelity obligations encompass such responsibilities as: troops should be properly trained and equipped; adequate medical and psychiatric treatment should be made available; aid in making the post-service transition to civilian life should be offered; if there is a military draft, it should be equitable; if there is a volunteer army, the troops should be treated as more than just mercenaries; strategic and tactical battle plans should be adequate.

The military context is not the only place where implied obligations are articulated. Recipients of farm subsidies, who have organized their lives around those subsidies (some of which date back to the 1930s), argue that there is some fidelity obligation to continue them—or if they are discontinued an obligation to phase them out gradually over a considerable period of time. Implied or inferred commitments surfaced in the summer of 2008 as the Fannie Mae and Freddie Mac organizations were caught up in the housing mortgage crisis. It became clear that many investors had presumed that these organizations and their assets were guaranteed by the government because the federal government had established and chartered these companies. No such guarantee existed, but this widespread assumption had influenced the decisions of many investors, and that in turn played a part in the fashioning of governmental financial relief for these organizations.

Implied fidelity is based on understandings of the purpose of government. In keeping with Alexander Hamilton's view that "the security of Property" is one of the "great objects of Government," many governments have made explicit commitments to protect individuals' rights to private property. But implied understandings often create presumptions about what those obligations to protect private property actually mean. When the U.S. Supreme

Court examined a government taking of private property in the landmark case Kelo vs. City of New London, some of the justices hearing the case made important distinctions between property owners who were landlords who rented out their holdings, and property owners who were residents with long-standing and familial ties to their homes. Justice Sandra Day O'Conner wrote, "Petitioner Wilhelmina Dery, for example, lives in a house on Walbach Street that has been in her family for over 100 years. She was born in the house in 1918; her husband, petitioner Charles Dery, moved into the house when they married in 1946. Their son lives next door with his family in the house he received as a wedding gift, and joins his parents in this suit. Two petitioners keep rental property in the neighborhood."[5]

If the only value implicated in this case was the legal protection of private property, there already existed an explicit commitment to all property owners, and all that was required was to interpret and apply that formal commitment. But clearly there was some kind of implied obligation at work here, in addition to the formal law. There was some kind of presumed commitment reflected in Justice O'Conner's opinion that drew a distinction between the treatment of different types of landowners. One commentator voiced this sense of a government obligation to keep faith with some of these residents, describing them as the ones who "stayed for decades, paying taxes, shoveling snow from their driveways, attending PTA meetings, raising money for the local Kiwanis Club and Veterans Day parades. Don't they deserve a reward for all that commitment?"[6] The answer to this question is not found in formal explicit commitments, but in one's understanding of implied obligations.

External Assumptions

Disagreement often surrounds the interpretations of explicit commitments that have been made, structural constraints, and the implied obligations that are discussed above. Even more contentious is the debate over a fourth type of obligation under the benchmark of fidelity: whether, and to what extent, a government should assume external values in the making and administration of public policy. "To assume" can mean to take upon oneself. Thus, the question can be posed as whether a government should take upon itself values, beliefs and priorities that have their source from beyond its borders. "Assumption" also says something about the nature of the obligations being identified here. "To assume" also means to suppose without verification or proof. This kind of obligation often operates as an asserted value that is accepted without being vetted critically and approved by independent parties.

Nations do ratify external norms by embodying them in statutes, treaties and constitutions. When that occurs, the norm has become a commitment that has been made, an explicit responsibility of the sort described above. For these assumed obligations, however, the meaning and force of the norms are not matters of explicit identification or formally approved standards. Instead they are more taken-for-granted, assumed as self-evident bases for deliberation and policy formulation.

Assumptions of external values are not the same as decisions to abide by external norms to achieve beneficial results. There is a difference between the question of whether and to what extent a nation should assume these external values as a matter of fundamental principle, and whether the external values should be assumed for pragmatic reasons. This difference points to a distinction between the external assumptions being raised here, and arguments about consequences, the topic discussed in the section on Benefit. On many occasions, decisions about accepting external norms are based on consequentialist arguments. Such arguments hold, for example, that we ought to treat foreigners in humane ways so that our citizens will be treated well by other governments. Or that America's power in the world (especially the "soft power," the ability to influence other countries through cultural, social and political strength, without resorting to the use of force) will be enhanced if we are viewed around the globe as a nation whose policies conform to an international moral consensus on key issues. Such pragmatic arguments about consequences surfaced on both sides of the discussion of the "torture memos" written in the Bush administration. Some opposition to these memos was based on the belief that the information gained through this kind of treatment of prisoners was unreliable. Other opponents worried that other nations would be more likely to torture Americans they held as prisoners, if the United States tortured the prisoners it held. These are important arguments, but they are arguments about the overall effectiveness of the practices, rather than about incorporating external norms about torture into our sense of fidelity. In this effectiveness-based opposition the appeal was to beneficial consequences that would flow from adhering to certain international moral norms, not a belief that these norms should be assumed by the U.S. government because of their very nature.

Assumptions of external values are not the same as having made explicit commitments to abide by external norms. Some commentators opposed the torture memos based on interpretations of U.S. legal obligations. The United States had signed treaties and joined international conventions. Official government conduct had endorsed general practices that are accepted as international law, actions that were believed to have created obligations that should guide policy making in the United States. These were obligations concerning the treatment of individuals abroad as well as people within our own borders. Through treaties, conventions and general practice the United States had explicitly bound itself to certain provisions of international law—the type of obligation described in the "commitments made" section above. The question was the precise meaning of those commitments that had been made.

The external assumptions being addressed here raise a different set of questions than those posed by effectiveness arguments, or by explicit commitments to international norms embraced in U.S. treaties. Should "a decent respect to the opinions of mankind," to use the words from the Declaration of Independence, be a factor in the formation of American policy? Should international norms that have not been explicitly adopted by a country play a role in the moral assessment of that nation's policies? Does the benchmark of fidelity extend its reach beyond a country's boundaries? In the same way that the U.S. government owes faithfulness to its own citizens and residents, does it also have a similar duty to the citizens of the world, to be faithful and true to humanitarian norms?

When international norms are assumed to be a valid basis for judging policies on the treatment of prisoners, opposition to the torture memos is then based on the simple proposition that the treatment is morally wrong. Judgments about the effectiveness of the enhanced interrogation techniques, or the meaning of obligations under international law, are not relevant to an assessment that assumes the validity of humanitarian values. Under that assumption, the government is obligated to treat all prisoners properly, in keeping with this external value.

One enduring source of international norms is the post-World War II Nuremberg trials. We speak of the Nuremberg legacy and principles, of the spirit of Nuremberg, and we do so in a way that implies that the precedent of those trials does indeed provide benchmarks for how the United States should conduct its affairs. But in any given case, a number of factors (the vagueness of humanitarian principles, the variety of sources of international norms, the lack of consensus about balancing national self-interest and moral principles) will combine to guarantee that these will be contentious matters for the foreseeable future. One test of our sincerity and consistency will be our willingness to define the role of international norms in the assessment of policy in the same way for ourselves that we expect for other countries.

Religion is another external source, in addition to international norms, for grounding obligations of fidelity. Some believers find the value of protecting innocent life in their religious tradition to constitute a basis for the government to prohibit abortions, although other believers in the same tradition do not agree. Similarly, adherents in a particular faith find teachings that provide a basis for abolishing the death penalty, although other adherents to the same faith are not convinced. Some believe that religious values support discrimination on the basis of sexual orientation; others believe just the opposite. There is often a lack of consensus about exactly what religious values mean for public policy assessments, but there is no doubt that such values inform the way in which many citizens think about relationships between the governors and the governed.

Perhaps the best-known religious statement on this relationship is the phrase attributed to Jesus of Nazareth in the synoptic gospels: Render unto Caesar the things that are Caesar's, and unto God the things that are God's.

This response to a question about whether Jews should pay taxes to the Roman occupation government establishes limits on the reach of secular authority. While this statement provides a religious foundation for recognizing an obligation by the government to respect those limits, it also appears to recognize a legitimate sphere of operation for government. On first impression, the appearance of Caesar's image on the coin of the day suggests that taxes should be paid. However, the proper scope of government suggested in Jesus' response is a matter of debate, especially in light of interpretations which hold that Jesus would have been familiar with scripture found in the Hebrew Bible which asserts that everything belongs to God—which ultimately leaves nothing for Caesar.

Identifying God's will as a source of obligation for governments is more than an affirmation that the values of a country's populace can appropriately be based upon their religious beliefs. Rather, it is an affirmation that adherence to God's will should be an external constraint on government action even if that faith is not embraced by the majority—or perhaps especially if it is not embraced by the majority. It may be that this divine law is not written into the structure of the government, as is the case with Sharia in Iran and Saudi Arabia, but it is argued that these obligations should still be assumed by those who are making and implementing policy.

The history of the United States is full of examples of relying on religious sources to guide government action. Advocates of this approach point to the Declaration of Independence, citing the familiar phrases "the separate and equal station to which the Laws of Nature and of Nature's God entitle them," and that all people are "endowed by their Creator with certain unalienable rights." A less-well known phrase identifies a standard of judgment external to the community itself, as the Continental Congress was "appealing to the supreme judge of the world for the rectitude of our intentions." Martin Luther King, Jr., in his Letter from Birmingham City Jail, made the case for a divine standard for judging governance. He wrote that he agreed with St. Augustine that "an unjust law is no law at all," employing this formulation: "A just law is a man-made law that squares with the moral law or the law of God. An unjust law is a code that is out of harmony with the moral law."[7] Evangelist Billy Graham addressed a Presidential Prayer Service in 1985: "There's a mandate that is higher than the ballot box, and it comes from God. We have a responsibility not only to all the people of America and to the people of the world, but also we have a great responsibility to the God of our fathers."[8]

There is disagreement about the extent to which a responsibility to God should make a difference in the way those who govern fulfill their other obligations. President Jimmy Carter addressed this point of contention when he was asked whether his Christian beliefs ever conflicted with his secular duties as President. His response betrays the ambivalence of many in power who have faced this question: "I have never believed that Jesus Christ would approve either abortions or the death penalty, but I obeyed such

Supreme Court decisions to the best of my ability, at the same time attempting to minimize what I considered to be their adverse impact."[9] Carter was walking a tightrope as he attempted to minimize the effect of such decisions without violating the Court's core intentions. Joseph Califano served as Carter's Secretary of Health, Education and Welfare, and he disagreed with Carter about how their personal moral beliefs should influence the way regulations were written to implement legislative acts. Califano thought that the President failed to appropriately exclude religious values when Carter attempted to fashion regulations in light of his own beliefs, concluding that Carter's personal religious views should not alter his duty to faithfully determine what Congress had intended and to write regulations accordingly.[10]

Not all conceptions of "higher law" are religious. Universal moral standards have been grounded in human reason or natural law and, as mentioned earlier, some of these have found their way into constitutional provisions. An understanding of fidelity accounts for the "reverence" attached to Constitutional rights. These are not just legal rights, which they are, but they also reflect a moral claim that the populace recognizes. American citizens believe that the Bill of Rights, for example, is a set of promises that have been made to protect rights that precede the establishment of any government. From the moral point of view, these are not fundamental rights because they are in the Constitution; they are in the Constitution because they are believed to be fundamental rights. The aspects of "higher law" that have been codified in the Constitution have become explicit commitments that the government has obligated itself to uphold. For many people, there are aspects of higher law that have not yet been so codified, and in those cases they recognize the existence of responsibilities of fidelity that should be assumed from this external source.

The Ideal of Public Service

An assessment of public policy on the basis of fidelity begins with an inquiry into whether there are existing commitments to be fulfilled. In cases in which a government's actions are found to be contrary to its commitments to those who will be affected by those actions, a concern about fidelity has been raised. The problem with fidelity is that it is mushy. The obligations are vague, imprecise and contested. The guidance for policy makers that is provided by structural requirements, presumed obligations and external assumptions is hazy, at best. Explicit commitments are more clear and certain, but these can be changed by those who are bound by them—and they often are changed as different circumstances arise or political winds shift. Statutes are repealed; regulations are altered; promises are regularly refined, clarified or updated. Even constitutions can be amended.

Obligations of fidelity lack the specificity of benefit and effectiveness, whose significance can often be quantified and presented in precise equations.

Fidelity often lacks the definitiveness of the benchmark of fairness which can be encapsulated in thumbnail slogans (provide equal opportunity, distribute equal shares, give people what they are willing to pay for). Even though Fidelity lacks clarity, precision or consensus, this concept does speak to a deep and central vision of the relationship between government and those who are governed. We call people who work for the government "public servants." There exists a vision that those who govern work for the people—or at least that they should do so. The people elect those who make policy. The people pay taxes; there is no government money except that which comes from the people. Those who are in power, who make policies and administer those policies, are in those positions to provide service to the public.

A gap always exists between the ideal of public service and the reality of political life. Sometimes the gap is so huge that it is difficult for us to take seriously these paragraphs. This kind of aspirational language is especially needed when policy decisions seem to be increasingly driven by concerns about re-election, contests of power and personal gain. Revisiting the lofty visions of public service is one of the few alternatives to surrendering to a cynical abdication that expects the worst of everyone involved in the policy process.

The concept of a fiduciary relationship captures the ideal of public service. A fiduciary relationship is one in which a person is under a duty to act for the benefit of another. Policy makers and administrators serve in this capacity. Lawyers and financial advisors are commonly thought of as being in fiduciary relationships with their clients. Just as lawyers and financial advisors have an obligation to act for the benefit of their clients, rather than serve their personal interests, so public servants are obligated to act on behalf of the public instead of pursuing their own interests. When those who make and implement policy accept their positions, they are making a commitment to fulfill this duty, to act for the benefit of the public they have chosen to serve.

Obligations of fidelity offer a way to keep the governors honest. These obligations provide a way to try to bridge the gulf that is reflected in language that speaks of the government as an "it" that is akin to an alien invader. Government takeovers (as we have heard discussed in recent debates about health care) are maligned as they present the image of the people losing control over their own lives. A robust sense of fidelity can help nurture the possibility that the people can use government as a tool to enhance control of their lives. When this can be accomplished, then despite the vagueness and imprecision, fidelity can occupy a significant place as tradeoffs are made among all of the benchmarks in the assessment of public policy.

Notes

1 Lon L. Fuller, *The Morality of Law*, rev. ed. (New Haven: Yale University Press, 1969).
2 Ibid., p. 53.

3 Ibid., p. 81.
4 For a sample of the debate, see Elizabeth Price Foley, *Liberty for All: Reclaiming Individual Privacy in a New Era of Public Morality* (New Haven: Yale University Press, 2006).
5 Kelo v. City of New London, 545 U.S. 469, 494–5 (O'Connor dissent).
6 Carla T. Main, *Bulldozed: "Kelo," Eminent Domain, and the American Lust for Land* (New York: Encounter Books, 2007), p. 150.
7 Martin Luther King, Jr., "Letter from Birmingham City Jail," in *Why We Can't Wait* (New York: Harper & Row, 1963), p. 82.
8 Billy Graham, "A Nation Under God," President Prayer Service, Washington National Cathedral, January 20, 1985. Quoted in Jon Meacham, *American Gospel: God, the Founding Fathers, and the Making of the Nation* (New York: Random House, 2006), p. 215. From Files of the Billy Graham Evangelistic Association.
9 Jimmy Carter, *Our Endangered Values: America's Moral Crisis* (New York: Simon and Schuster, 2005), p. 57.
10 Joseph A. Califano, Jr., *Governing America: An Insider's Report from the White House and the Cabinet* (New York: Simon and Schuster, 2007).

7 Ownership of Problems
Legitimacy

The Legitimacy benchmark is designed to guide decisions about which areas of our lives properly fall within the range of government action, and which do not. Every problem is not the government's problem. The focus of this discussion is on moral limits to the reach of governance—not legal or constitutional limits. From an ethical point of view, an action taken by a duly constituted government is not necessarily a legitimate exercise of power. Moral boundaries and legal boundaries have not always coincided, nor should they always do so.

Prohibition serves as an illustration. The Eighteenth Amendment to the U.S. Constitution provided: "After one year from the ratification of this article the manufacture, sale, or transportation of intoxicating liquors within, the importation thereof into, or the exportation thereof from the United States and all territory subject to the jurisdiction thereof for beverage purposes is hereby prohibited." That amendment was passed on December 3, 1917, with all of the appropriate legal and constitutional procedures for amending the Constitution having been properly observed. All of the required votes were taken; all of the required voting margins were secured. From a legal point of view, the action taken was a legitimate one. Many citizens, however, continued to oppose the action as an illegitimate intrusion into their private lives or as an illegitimate restriction of individual and economic liberties. Arguments that were based on a moral standard for legitimacy continued to challenge this use of governmental power until the policy was overturned with the passage of the Twenty-first Amendment in 1933.

Another illustration of the difference between ethical judgments and legal judgments are the cases in which citizens take a position on the morality of an activity, while believing that it is illegitimate for that moral judgment to become the substance of public policy. For four decades, the American populace has been split on the morality of abortion. Over the years, the percentage of Americans who personally believe that abortion is wrong has fallen within the 50–60 percent range. Yet, in a 2013 NBC News/Wall Street Journal poll, 70 percent of those surveyed said they would not like to see Roe v. Wade overturned. The percentage answering the same way to a similar question in a Pew Research Center poll was 63 percent. Many American citizens who think abortion is wrong do not believe the government should enforce that moral judgment by repealing the law of the land that protects the liberty to choose in these circumstances.

If moral analysis and legal analysis are distinguishable in this way, then the question becomes one of determining where the difference lies: which aspects of our lives are properly subject to government actions and which are not? The benchmark of Legitimacy provides the criteria for making judgments about which public policies represent legitimate exercises of government power. The underlying assumption for such a principle is that there are some matters that are not proper subjects for legislation or government regulation. This assumption is a valid one for observers who can think of both a subject that is appropriately the concern of policy makers (e.g., murder) and a subject that is not appropriately the concern of policy makers (e.g., breaking a commitment to read a passage of scripture to a child at bedtime). Anyone who believes that every problem is not necessarily the government's problem should develop some basis for deciding which problems are the government's problems and which are not. Amy Gutmann and Dennis Thompson have described these "principles of preclusion" as serving the purpose of determining which policies "deserve a place on the political agenda in the sense of being a legitimate subject for legislation."[1]

Good reasons should be given for concluding that a problem is a proper subject for public policy intervention. The criteria that we use to draw such distinctions reflect our views about the proper scope of state action. In recent decades it has not been unusual to hear Republicans present this one issue as representative of the differences between the philosophies of the two major political parties in the United States. These G.O.P. speakers have repeatedly expressed the view that Democrats, when addressing a social problem, are too quick to jump to proposing government solutions. Examples that are cited include gay rights legislation, regulating business, government provision of health care, and environmental protection legislation. They argue that Republicans want less government interference in the lives of citizens. They are more willing to rely on private efforts and individual initiatives in solving social ills than their Democrat colleagues.

Democrats, on the other hand, have attempted to turn this characterization on its head, arguing that it is the Republican Party that has taken positions that reflected unwarranted government intervention in the lives of citizens—citing as examples such issues as abortion, the regulation of private conduct between consenting adults, the use of contraception, intervention in medical decisions like those in the Teri Shivo case, the federal government overriding states' approval of the use of marijuana for medical purposes, and invasion of privacy in fighting crime. Setting a limit on the range of legitimate government activity is a common practice, but different people draw that line in very different ways on different issues.

While a finding of illegitimacy can be a telling blow against a particular policy, a finding of legitimacy does not mean that a particular policy is desirable. A determination that a problem is one that can be legitimately addressed by government only opens the door for the evaluation of policy options in light of other principles. Thus, for example, one can argue that it is legitimate for government to impose sanctions for the commission of crimes against others but still be opposed to a specific set of mandatory sentencing guidelines. Similarly one can agree that it is a legitimate exercise of governmental power to criminalize the use of marijuana or to prohibit the manufacture of non-returnable bottles and yet argue against such policies on other grounds.

In the following section, I identify nine different standards that have been used for making judgments about legitimacy. This list is a real hodge podge, reflecting the widely varying ways in which legitimacy arguments are made. Some of these items are substantive criteria; others more procedural. Some focus on concerns about individual actions, others on societal well-being, and still others on morality. Strong advocates exist for each of these standards, and all of them can be found in our everyday discussions about when government action is legitimate. This chapter concludes with some thoughts about how we can make sense of these disparate approaches to legitimacy.

Moral Assessments of Legitimacy

Harm to Others

John Stuart Mill has given us a good starting place for thinking about legitimacy as a moral issue. Mill provided a simple, succinct statement that embodies one of the most widely-expressed standards of legitimacy: "[T]he only purpose for which power can be rightfully exercised over any member of a civilized community, against his will, is to prevent harm to others."[2] The state can legitimately interfere with the liberty of any person only in the cause of protecting other individuals.

Mill was a utilitarian. His ethical theory was not the "Hair" musical philosophy of doing whatever you want, as long as you don't hurt anybody. He believed that moral acts were those that produced the greatest amount of good for the greatest number of people. However, he clearly distinguished between his moral views about the actions an individual should choose, and the grounds that would be required for the legal coercion of that person. For Mill, moral judgments about what is wise or right do supply a basis for attempting to persuade a person to act in certain ways, but not for forcing him to act in desirable ways. Mill did recognize some exceptions to a universal application of his Harm to Others criteria. He did favor a more extensive reach for government in the cases of children and what he called "barbarians" and those in "backward states of society." Other than in such exceptional cases, though, the legitimate scope of any government activity that limits liberty, invades privacy or imposes penalties is restricted to actions that harm other persons.

Stating such a formula is, of course, only the beginning point. Defining "harm" is open to a variety of interpretational differences. Does harm mean only physical harm? Does it include economic or psychological damage? Harm can be caused in varying degrees and surely not *any* harm is appropriate for governmental response. What about indirect harm or harm caused when one fails to act? Mill himself uses this standard to argue that a person may legitimately be compelled by law to perform acts for the benefit of others such as testifying in court, bearing a fair share of the national defense, and acting to save another person who is in danger.

There are contemporary versions of the view of legitimacy developed by Mill. A typical starting point is a belief in the sovereignty of the individual, a conviction that each person possesses a protected zone in which he should be free from encroachment by others, especially by government. The legitimate role for government is to protect each of us from encroachment by others, to allow us the space to pursue our own interests and projects. The focus is on liberty rights, and government is justified in exercising its coercive powers only to protect the liberty that is necessary for individuals to control their own lives. Efforts by the state to act more expansively, for example to coerce individuals to act morally, are simply illegitimate.

The strict use of a Mill-type harm-to-others criterion for legitimacy would rule out many of the laws and regulations that have become a common feature of our society. Arguably such "victimless crimes" as the use of drugs could be beyond the proper scope of governmental power. Requiring the use of motorcycle helmets and seat belts in automobiles can only indirectly, if at all, be shown to be an appropriate way to prevent harm to other persons. Government programs that redistribute wealth or provide a variety of benefits and services would be suspect under this understanding of legitimacy.

Harm to Self

A second reason that can be given for legitimating state action is paternalism—preventing people from harming themselves. A demonstration of the harmful effects of an activity is still required under this standard, but the harm to be considered includes harm that an actor does to himself, not just to others. Laws requiring the use of seat belts, regulating the rate structure of credit cards, or prohibiting the sale of ineffective drugs are examples of policies whose legitimacy has been supported by paternalistic arguments.

Paternalistic concerns can be divided between consent-based paternalism (so-called soft paternalism) and welfare-based paternalism (hard paternalism). Legitimating a consent-based paternalistic policy entails a judgment that the affected decisions are not truly free or informed—and, further, that the person whose liberty is being restricted by government action could accept the goal of the policy if her decisions were unimpaired. The purpose of consent-based paternalism is to remedy the problem caused when persons are making choices under duress, coercion or without adequate and accurate information. The intent is to create a situation in which they can make free, informed decisions or, failing that, to make the choices for them that they would have made if such a situation could have been created. Regulations governing financial transactions, requirements that some consumer products carry warning labels, and permitting medical treatment decisions without the expressed consent of the patient in certain circumstances are examples of such policies.

Welfare-based paternalism, on the other hand, is more directly concerned with protecting people from harm, even if it is a harm they would freely choose. If prevention of harm is the moral basis for the harm-to-others standard, it is argued, why would that moral basis not also apply to harm persons cause themselves? The argument that there are limits to the amount of harm we should allow people to cause themselves is used to support policies prohibiting people from selling themselves into slavery, donating vital organs, or engaging in certain risk-taking behaviors that appear to be freely chosen. This type of pure paternalism does not concern itself with consent-based issues such as whether the individual is competent to make the choice or understands the possible consequences of her actions. Rather, welfare-based paternalism calls for a free, informed, fully-competent adult to be restrained by the government simply and solely to keep her from suffering a self-imposed harm. Thus, for example, while a consent-based paternalism might call for warning labels on tobacco or marijuana products, a welfare-based paternalism might ban the use of the substances.

Offense to Others

A variation on the Harm to Others criterion is the standard of Offense to Others. Offense to others is concerned with conduct that produces mental states in other persons that are so unpleasant that legal protection from such conduct is legitimate. This criterion for legitimacy could be used to argue in favor of restrictions on activities such as pornography, desecration of religious symbols, the mutilation of corpses, public nudity, and obscenity. Joel Feinberg has suggested that decisions about when opposition to offensive behavior legitimates government action should employ a balancing test that weighs the seriousness of the resulting offense against such factors as the importance of the conduct to the offending party and the availability of alternatives in which the conduct would be less offensive.[3]

The offense-to-others standard serves to legitimate governmental policy only when a particular individual is offended by exposure to the conduct of another, similar to the way that a person can be harmed by the conduct of another. This exposure to the offending act is an important feature for this benchmark. The principle does not extend to a person who is offended by the idea of something happening that he believes is morally wrong, when the activity occurs in private and beyond his view. Dissatisfaction with immoral activity that takes place in private, to which the offended person has not been exposed, has at times been used to legitimate state action. However, this kind of government action invokes not the offense-to-others criterion, but the different standard of the enforcement of morality, which is discussed in the next section.

These first three criteria (Harm to Others, Harm to Self, and Offense to Others) reflect a general caution, if not a hostility, toward the role of government in regulating our lives. This restricted approach favors a government that reaches far enough into our lives to protect us from each other, and on special occasions perhaps to protect us from ourselves, but not so far as to become a threat to our liberty. This "watchdog state" is a minimalist state, primarily concerned with enabling each individual to pursue his or her interests without interference from others. These standards most often undergird the criminal law and certain regulatory aspects of the state. There are, however, more far-reaching ways to think about the nature and role of government, and we will now turn to some standards that embody this more expansive view of legitimate government action.

Enforcement of Morality

One of the most expansive concepts of government legitimacy views the state as an instrument to be used in the enforcement of morality. This approach sees public policy as a tool that the community can use to give effect to its basic moral beliefs: an appropriate role for government is to enforce morality on its citizens. In a democracy, this standard for the legitimacy of state action can easily become an expression of legal moralism, the belief that the majority has a right (even a duty) to dictate how everyone should live. Legal moralism holds that it can be morally legitimate to regulate certain types of behavior not because they cause harm or offense to anyone, but simply because they are immoral. A landmark statement of such a position was presented by Lord Patrick Devlin in his lecture and essay, *The Enforcement of Morals.*[4] Devlin concluded that society has the right to pass judgment on matters of morals and that it further has the right to use "the weapon of law" to enforce its judgments. He asserts that there are certain moral principles that society insists be observed and that the function of the criminal law is to enforce moral principles.

This connection between morality and law grows out of a conviction that the legitimacy of state action depends upon its conformity to higher law, whether it be natural law or divine law. The natural law tradition, for example, has affirmed certain basic moral laws that have their origin in the nature of things or in theological versions that have been decreed by God. The legitimacy of governance depends upon its conformity to those natural or divine laws.

At one level, the position that public policy legitimately enforces the community's morality seems unobjectionable. What is the alternative? A position that legitimate policy is that which contradicts the community's view of right and wrong? On the other hand, however, there exists an understandable caution toward morally-inspired laws and legally-enforced morality in our society. The concerns are expressed in a variety of different bromides that draw lines between the role of morality and the role of law: *Law addresses public matters; morality deals with private affairs. Law is a necessary evil, providing the minimum structure needed for social existence, while morality supplies the content for our aspirations to do what is good, right, and true. Law seeks the lowest common denominator in regulating behavior; morality describes the best for which we should strive.* In these and other formulations, citizens express a conviction that the distinctive roles of law and morality should not be blended. Whether it is "liberals" wanting to get government out of our bedrooms or "conservatives" opposing the enforcement of gay-rights agendas, the sentiment that government should not be in the morality business is easy to find.

Efforts to use public policy to enforce morality must, of course, rest on a selection of the particular morality to be enforced. For Devlin, the choice was simple. He advocated the imposition of a wide range of values on all citizens simply and solely because those standards reflected the morality of the majority. However, for most advocates of the enforcement of morality the touchstone is not what most people in a society believe but rather the true morality, the one truly grounded in divine or natural law. Indeed, the most energetic efforts to use government to enforce moral values usually come from those who fear that the majority has become an unreliable guide to truth and virtue.

Harm to Society

A closer reading of Devlin yields a second thesis that is more moderate than the proposition that government is free to enforce any position simply because it is moral.[5] In this alternative reading, Devlin recognizes a limit to the legitimate use of governmental authority, drawing an analogy to state suppression of treason: a collective moral judgment can be enforced only if society is threatened in a fundamental way. Some kind of common morality is seen to be the cement that holds a society together, a binding force that is required for the existence of any society. Thus, for Devlin a community can use the government to preserve its morality in the same way that it uses the government to protect the community from external threats. Policies enforcing morality can be used to protect society from internal disintegration. This position shifts the discussion from an enforcement of moral standards because they are right, to an assessment of the effects of certain behavior.

The issue of legitimacy becomes an empirical question in this more moderate scheme. Which features of the public morality are essential to the continued existence of that society? We can expect differences in judgment in response to this question. For example, Devlin argued that policies prohibiting deviation from accepted sexual morality were legitimate, because he thought such behavior would cause societal disintegration. One of Devlin's critics, H. L. A. Hart, offered this response to Devlin's argument: "As a proposition of fact, it is entitled to no more respect than the Emperor Justinian's statement that homosexuality was the cause of earthquakes."[6] Such disagreements in judgment will focus on the evidence regarding the *effects* on a society's existence of allowing, prohibiting, or requiring certain behavior—as distinct from the standard that morality should be enforced for its own sake. The difference between the enforcement-of-morality and the harm-to-society standards can be seen clearly in recent debates regarding gays in the military. A harm-to-society approach carefully examines the evidence concerning whether the enlistment of gays and lesbians has negative consequences for the effectiveness of our armed services—and is open to the possibilities that they might or might not. Those who wish to make their decisions based on the moral evaluations of homosexuality (positive or negative) have no need to wait for such evidence to form their conclusions.

The common thread in these two positions illustrated in Devlin's work is that public policy can be used in an affirmative way, supporting a specific morality and ensuring that societal institutions and practices reflect that morality. The legitimate scope of policy ranges beyond the prevention of identifiable harms or offenses to a more active regulation that can reach into all aspects of individuals' lives. Knowing what policies are legitimate is first a matter of knowing what the "correct" morality is—not a trivial matter in a modern, pluralistic society. Unless the true or proper morality is simply a question of public opinion (an issue to be taken up shortly), any form of legal moralism can finally be viewed as valid only to the extent that an observer accepts as authoritative the content of the particular morality being espoused.

Enhance Virtue

Robert George has developed a morals-based approach to justifying government policy that focuses on helping people establish and preserve a virtuous character. Whereas the enforcement-of-morality legitimacy standard is a matter of commanding outward conformity to moral rules (using the power of the state to punish those who act immorally), George emphasizes an interest in helping people "make themselves" moral, in part by providing an environment that educates citizens about right and wrong, and that preserves a moral ecology in which people make their choices. He writes: "I shall argue that sound politics and good law *are* concerned with helping people to lead morally upright and valuable lives, and, indeed, that a good political society may justly bring to bear the coercive power of public authority to provide people with some protection from the corrupting influences of vice."[7] The point is that a community's moral ecology provides a basis for laws and policies that exert an important educative influence on the formation of values.[8] This shaping of moral habits occurs both when the law speaks (explicit moral teaching) and when it fails to speak (implying assent to or a legitimation of unregulated acts).

We recognize this formation of society's moral values in the changes to our public schools. We expect those government institutions to socialize our children into a community that values such things as honesty, industry and fairness. As for adults, we embrace policies that send signals about desirable behavior, such as making environmentally-sound choices or economically-beneficial decisions. We act on a belief that government can exert an important educative influence in the development of sound moral values.

The key in fashioning public policy that enhances virtue is knowing with some certainty what constitutes virtue, what is right and wrong. In a pluralistic society, in which there is often considerable disagreement about what morality requires on certain issues, empowering government to make those judgments will be a contested matter. Approval of a government action to enhance virtue largely depends on personal agreement with the specific choice. For example, many of those who want government to encourage abstinence may at the same time oppose government incentives that encourage environmental protection. The emphasis in this approach is on providing support and aid to those wanting to make moral choices. However, if one result is that some citizens find their own choices being undermined by the coercive power of government, the outcome for those citizens may not seem much different than an enforcement-of-morality regime in which conformity to a set of moral rules is commanded.

Promote the Common Good

Another positive view of the nature and scope of public policy is associated with the rise of the welfare state. This approach deems as legitimate those policies which promote the common good. It is, after all, a provision of the preamble to our Constitution that states that one purpose of forming this union was to "promote the general Welfare." The right to pursue happiness, set forth in the Declaration of Independence, can be understood not as "the negative right of individuals to be protected by government *from* something; rather it was the positive right to be engaged *in* something, the right to pursue the public good in the public realm."[9] Thus, the state can aid and assist the citizenry in this pursuit, working for the common good of all. Government can act to identify the community's good, and any policies that further these ends would be legitimate. This criterion legitimizes the use of government to provide directly a range of goods and services. Such programs as Social Security, food stamps, Medicaid and worker's compensation are examples of policies that aim to improve the general welfare.

Arguments supporting the use of this expansive common good standard typically reject the perceived individualistic bias of the more constrained approaches to legitimating government action, approaches which stress the transcendence of the individual over the community. Charles Fried, however, has constructed a more expansive legitimation of government action that begins with the value of individual autonomy. He emphasizes the point that the valuing of one person's autonomy should lead to the valuing of all persons' autonomy. Believing that it is wrong for us to be indifferent to the autonomy of others, he shifts the focus from the liberty of the solitary individual to the needs of all individuals. A moral grounding is provided for policy making that provides goods to citizens to meet their basic needs: "A person has a claim on his fellows to a standard package of basic or essential goods . . . housing, education, health care, food: i.e., the social (or decent) minimum—if by reasonable efforts he cannot earn enough to produce this minimum for himself."[10] If autonomy can be exercised only when basic needs are met, then providing a minimum of such goods to those who cannot secure them on their own would be a legitimate government function.

Those who believe that serving the common good is a legitimate government function begin with the welfare of society as a whole. Their emphasis is on the interdependence of all members of a community, and on the ethically permissible, if not ethically obligatory, use of the institutions of governance to advance that welfare. From that base, the values of altruism, duty toward others, and a sense of community are offered as antidotes to the moral indifference and callous self-interest that are seen to be growing problems in the United States.

Enact the Public Will

Many conversations about the legitimacy of government action sooner or later turn to the topic of the will of the people. Particularly in a democracy, there is a generalized sense that judging the legitimacy of public policies has something to do with determining whether that policy has popular support. In one way or another, community values play a role in each of the standards of legitimacy that have been described so far, whether it is a matter of determining which morality to enforce, what constitutes the common good, or how we identify the harms and offenses that are worth preventing at the cost of restricting liberty. Often the criterion of public support is used in combination with one or more of the other criteria; for example, a policy is legitimate if it prevents harm to others and is supported by the community. However, it is not a simple task to move from that generalized sense that the community's choices count to more precise understandings of the role that the public should play in legitimizing government policies.

According to this kind of legitimacy criterion, public policy is legitimate as long as it is an expression of the will of the community. The complementary position would also be true: the implementation of policies that are clearly contrary to the public will would constitute illegitimate exercises of power. The argument for a connection between the preferences of the people and the actions of government is an appealing one, but it can be understood in different ways. A widely-accepted democratic formulation is that the will of the majority should rule. Consider two other formulations of the relationship between the public will and policy making that have also been put forth for our use: that policies should reflect a "general societal consensus"; or that legitimate policies reflect a "nearly universal social consensus."

Reviewing only these three positions uncovers a problem that must be addressed. Is the public-will standard merely that of majority sentiment, or "general" consensus, or "nearly universal" consensus? For a policy to be legitimate according to the public will criteria, is popular support of 50 percent plus one adequate, or is a more substantial test required? Even if the requirement is one of consensus, is a temporary consensus at any point in time enough or should there be a concern for the public will over time?

Choosing any of these standards poses problems. If conflicts should not be resolved by government until a national consensus has emerged, some of the most important and critical problems facing our community will go unaddressed. The requirement of a nearly universal consensus delivers the weapon of the veto to very small minorities. In addition, this position ignores the appropriately well-worn phrase that "Not to decide is to decide." The decision not to implement new policies means that existing policies will continue to govern our lives. The policy decisions of the past are, in effect, deemed to be legitimate even if they, too, now fail to command a societal consensus. Whether the issue is abortion, environmental pollution or economic malaise, a refusal on the part of government to act until there is a clear national consensus means that policy will exist by default. The United States was approaching a "fiscal cliff" at the end of 2012, as large tax increases and even larger spending cuts were scheduled to take effect because of prior congressional action. While there were very few advocates for driving off that cliff, the lack of consensus about how to avoid that result created the very real possibility that those increases and cuts, at one time considered unimaginable, could by default go into effect—creating a fiscal outcome that virtually no one supported. And in 2013, that was precisely what happened.

If, on the other hand, the criterion is not a difficult-to-achieve consensus but simply majoritarian sentiment, a new set of problems emerges. It is difficult to defend the position that any act of Congress is an illegitimate act of governance if it has the support of only 49 percent of the public. Such a view faces practical problems as well as theoretical problems in a representative democracy. Theoretically, this exclusive focus on understanding legislative action as an expression of the popular will ignores a second duty of legislators—to act in the service of the public. The dual obligations of representative legislators include playing an independent role in the assessment and resolution of societal problems. This independent role requires a deliberative response, with policy choices being based on independently held values and knowledge, not merely reflecting what appear to be the preferences of bare majorities at a particular point in time.

More issues are raised when we realize that most problems can be addressed by a variety of policy responses. When multiple alternatives are available for consideration, it is commonly the case that no single option is the preferred option for an absolute majority of the populace. While political theorists agree that democracy has something to do with majority rule, many have questioned whether we can identify anything that could be called "the public will," and have concluded that a requirement that all policy actions reflect majority consent in order to be legitimate is often simply impossible to meet.

Measurement of the public will constitutes another practical problem. If public opinion polls are to be believed, significant swings in citizen sentiment over a short period of time occur frequently. Thus, a public opinion poll approach to the public will as a keystone of legitimacy would yield results that would make congressional action on a matter legitimate in one week, but could make Presidential concurrence on the same matter a week later illegitimate. Do we rely on expert pollsters to analyze and interpret complex and inconsistent polling results and tell us what the public wants? Or do we defer to legislatures, granting those representative bodies the authority to divine the public will as they make laws?

The shifting of public opinion poses a problem not only for measurement, but for identifying the nature of the public will that should undergird policy decisions. The perhaps fleeting majoritarian sentiment about an issue on a particular day is a different animal than a long-term societal consensus that has persisted over time. A majority vote by a legislative body that is based on transient moral fashion that contradicts a community's long-held moral commitment could be seen to be morally illegitimate. On the other hand, the community's morality does change. The balancing of current societal standards against long-range historical views of the community's moral heritage is a never-ending process in the examination of the relationship between policy and its legitimization by the public's will.

Perfect the Marketplace

One view of the proper role of government is that the state should act to put into effect the private preferences of individuals as expressed by their willingness to pay for those results. In some ways, this approach is another version of the legitimacy standard of enforcing the public will. However, this distinctive approach does not resort to public opinion polls, referenda, legislative findings, or other mechanisms for determining the public will. Rather, an economic free market is held to be the mechanism that reveals public preferences.

The presupposition of this approach is that a democratic government legitimately acts when it produces outcomes that reflect the preferences of individual citizens. Policy is legitimate, therefore, to the extent that it mirrors the aggregate preferences of autonomous citizens. Thus, the proper role of government is to let the free market work. Since we do not live in an ideal world, there is also a legitimate role for government intervention, but only when market corrections are necessary (addressing problems such as imperfect information, free riders, or the imposition of externalities on third parties) or when markets are not available for public goods (for example, public health, safety or environmental quality). When the government does act in this corrective way, "public policy should act to mimic the outcomes competitive markets . . . would achieve, were such markets possible."[11]

Why is it desirable to keep the state away from the operation of the free market? The answer is that the market is presumed to be the most efficient mechanism for providing the benefits that citizens want. Government intrusion is deemed to be legitimate only when the market fails to provide for those benefits in an efficient way. Thus, legitimacy is dictated by one's presuppositions about the effectiveness with which benefit is attained by the public. Advocates of the other approaches to legitimacy could ask: Do we have aspirations that are decidedly moral commitments that we want the state to support but that cannot adequately be expressed in market terms? Is there a role for political participation and communal deliberation that can educate and elevate public opinion so that the governing process is more than simply gratifying individual, pre-existing preferences?

Sorting Through the Options

This chapter has presented brief descriptions of several approaches to determining which policies represent legitimate uses of the power of the state. Nine different ethical criteria have been identified here, but deciding which standard is appropriate is not as easy as picking a number from the list. The process, rather, is likely to be one of continuing refinement, adjustment and revision—a process like the pursuit of reflective equilibrium described in Chapter 2. First, while each of the nine can be summed up in a capsule statement, the appropriation of any one of these standards requires the definition of multiple terms and the discovery of nuances in application. Second, these criteria are not necessarily incompatible. One of these may be seen to be most appropriate in one arena (such as criminal law), while another may be most appropriate in another arena (regulating financial transactions). A third option is to adopt exceptions, stipulations, or combine features of different standards into new hybrid creations.

The process of sorting through these possibilities can be aided by dividing these nine standards into two groups, and subdividing each of those two into two sub-groups. The first division is between the criteria that are based on consequences, and those that are not. Falling into the first group of those that are effects-based standards, are the standards that focus on preventing negative outcomes (Harm to Others, Harm to Self, Offense to Others, Harm to Society), and those that focus on achieving positive outcomes (Promote the Common Good, Enhance Virtue). In the second group of those that are not effects-based standards are the two sub-categories of those that are essentially majoritarian in nature (Enact the Public Will, Perfect the Marketplace), and the morality-based criteria of the Enforcement of Morality.

This division is illustrated in this outline:

I. Effects-Based
    A. Negative Focus
        Harm to Others
        Harm to Self
        Offense to Others
        Harm to Society
    B. Positive Focus
        Promote the Common Good
        Enhance Virtue
II. Not Effects-Based
    A. Majoritarian
        Enact the Public Will
        Perfect the Marketplace
    B. Morality-Based
        Enforcement of Morality

The starting place for sorting through these options is the negative effects based standards, particularly the harm to others criteria. If there is any unanimity in our community discourse and in the professional literature, it lies in the legitimacy of government preventing one person from harming another. Thus, criminal codes regulate behavior among individuals, and those who violate those regulations are punished. Discussions of legitimacy quickly move beyond this base to issues such as the types and amount of harm that should be regulated, and then on to the other negative-effects standards: are there types of offensive behavior that should also be regulated? Should concerns about preventing harm expand to the paternalistic regulation of self-destructive behavior? Should harm to societal institutions receive the same kind of treatment as harm to individuals in some cases?

If we as a community want to prevent harmful acts and suffering, we should give serious consideration to a governmental role under the positive effects-based criteria, whether it be direct governmental action to promote the common good (feeding the hungry, treating the sick, clothing the poor), or to create a climate in which individuals are more likely to act in such beneficial ways (enhancing virtue). Harm occurs from acts of omission as well as commission. Harmful acts include collective decisions about the use of resources and opportunities, in addition to individual actions to inflict direct harm to others. Thus, a full assessment of the legitimate ways in which a government can address the well-being of its citizens should include an examination of goods and services that can provide beneficial results for individuals and society. We can instantly call to mind a range of times in which government has provided precisely this kind of assistance: relief along the Gulf of Mexico coast after an oil spill or a hurricane, free or low cost medical clinics, public education, an interstate highway system, national parks. The questions are what, when and how. When is it legitimate for government to act to provide which goods and services, and in what ways?

Moving from the effects-based standards, we can look at the majoritarian criteria, which place control in the hands of the public. To what extent should the assessment of the legitimacy of government action be based on what the people want, whether the populace expresses that will politically as citizens (the enact the public will standard) or economically as consumers (perfecting the marketplace standard)? Can a majoritarian standard stand alone as a sufficient basis for determining legitimacy? Such a position would assert that it is legitimate for the government to do whatever the people want it to do, as revealed by personal economic preferences, at the ballot box, or in public opinion polls. The problem with this position is that it conflates an acceptable proposition—that popular governance is the best political process—with a dubious proposition—that the majority always knows what is right. We should resist the notion that popular opinion is always the best guide for all matters of value related to government action. Historical counter-examples quickly come to mind: popularly supported enslavement of millions, decimation of indigenous peoples, and the prosecution of aggressive wars of conquest. Each citizen has a responsibility to develop his or her own standards for assessing the proper reach of public policy. And the sources for such standards are found in the other criteria.

The majoritarian criteria, however, can be important components of hybrid standards that individuals can develop. So, for example, one could develop a standard that it is legitimate for the government to prevent harm to others, as long as the harm is one that is recognized as an appropriate target by the public. Or that it is legitimate for the government to promote the public good, as long as the methods for doing so are restricted to those that perfect the marketplace. Before giving carte blanche to this kind of deference to majoritarian preferences, however, a citizen should give careful thought to occasions in which he or she would want to swim against the stream, to insist that certain government actions approved by the majority are illegitimate, and to attempt to change public opinion.

The remaining standard in the list of nine is the enforcement of morality. All of the other standards are based in morality in one way or another, drawing on beliefs about what is good and right. A distinctive feature of the enforcement-of-morality criteria is its emphasis on the legitimacy of using the government as an instrument to impose one view of what is good and right, irrespective of the public will. (In fact, a desire to enforce adherence to a particular morality is sometimes the strongest when the public is least inclined to follow those moral norms without government coercion.) When evaluating the advocacy of a position of this sort, the critical inquiry is whether the speaker's appeal is based on a view that the majority thinks his position is right, or that his position is right no matter what the majority thinks.

This enforcement-of-morality standard also differs from the effects-based standards in that it is not concerned with beneficial effects that might flow from policies, other than the desired conformity with that set of moral values. Thus, there is no place for discussions about whether the policy would work, or what the consequences of the policy might be. The enforcement-of-morality approach in a modern democratic society is difficult to justify. Strictly speaking, the claim is that it is legitimate for the government to act to enforce the morality of a minority segment of the population, regardless of the preferences of the majority, or any evidence that the resulting policy would provide any beneficial consequences for the community. Whether it's libertarians on the right, populists in the West, or progressives who celebrate tolerance and diversity, Americans resist that kind of regulation of our lives.

Do we want government to prevent people from harming others? Sometimes, yes. Do we want government to prevent people from harming themselves, even if only by requiring warning labels on dangerous products? Sometimes, yes. Do we want government to prevent people from offending others, from doing harm to important societal institutions, to enhance our societal welfare, to give expression to the will of the people? For all of these, sometimes, yes. Do we want government to enforce adherence to a particular moral code, even when *none* of these other purposes have been served? The answer may be never.

While this book treats legitimacy as a benchmark that is distinct from the others, there is also a question about whether legitimacy is indeed an independent principle. Legitimacy has been addressed here on its own terms, independent of any judgment about the desirability of a specific proposal. For our judgments about legitimacy to have any independent standing, we must be able to think of cases in which we would find a type of government action to be legitimate, even though we would oppose the adoption of that policy on other grounds. For example, you could conclude that it is legitimate for the government to provide universal health care, even if you opposed the policy because you think it would be an inefficient use of resources. We should also attempt to imagine instances in which we would doubt the legitimacy of government action, even when we believed that the resulting policies would be morally desirable on other grounds. For example, you could believe that it was illegitimate for the government to prohibit the sale of cigarettes, even though you would favor such a policy because of the benefit it would provide to the nation's health. This kind of search for clarity and consistency can help us find principled bases for our judgments.

The development of a comprehensive scheme for judging the legitimacy of all types of government action can be a matter of building from the ground up, of accumulating wisdom and perspective from a large number of individual judgments. Sometimes judgments about legitimacy are rendered in the negative: e.g., the state should not invade the privacy of consenting adults. Such negative starting points should be taken seriously. A citizen may arrive at a moral position which is something like: I don't know that I can specify a comprehensive, coherent philosophy that delineates what a government can legitimately do, but I do know that one thing it should not do is prohibit private acts between free, informed consenting adults.

In the interest of consistency and sincerity, anyone who makes such a statement should be pressed further. These types of judgments often are voiced in response to a particular case. Other cases should be brought into view to determine whether the individual would, indeed, object to *any* prohibition of *any* private act between consenting adults. Often, the result of this kind of exercise will be the addition of qualifications or greater specifications—e.g., that no physical harm is done. This testing not only leads to refinements in the initial judgment, but also can enhance an understanding of the general standards that produce the judgment. It is through a continual pressing of this sort, on a variety of different issues and topics, that we can move toward the formulation of a more comprehensive, consistent approach to judging the legitimacy of all types of government policy.

Notes

1 Amy Gutmann and Dennis Thompson, "Moral Conflict and Political Consensus," *Ethics*, vol. 101 (October 1990), p. 64.
2 John Stuart Mill, *On Liberty* (Chicago: Henry Regnery Co., 1955; 1859), p. 13.
3 Joel Feinberg, *Offense to Others* (New York: Oxford University Press, 1985). The other volumes in this series are also pertinent to the issues addressed in this discussion of legitimacy: *Harm to Others, Harm to Self*, and *Harmless Wrongdoing*.
4 Patrick Devlin, *The Enforcement of Morals* (London: Oxford University Press, 1965), pp. 1–25.
5 The distinction between these extreme and moderate theses is identified and discussed in H.L.A. Hart, *Law, Liberty and Morality* (Stanford, CA: Stanford University Press, 1963), pp. 48–52.
6 Ibid., p. 50.
7 Robert P. George, *Making Men Moral: Civil Liberties and Public Morality* (Oxford: Clarendon Press, 1993), p. 20.
8 Christopher Wolfe, "Public Morality and the Modern Supreme Court," *American Journal of Jurisprudence*, vol. 45 (2000), pp. 68–9.
9 Christopher F. Mooney, *Public Virtue: Law and the Social Character of Religion* (Notre Dame, IN: University of Notre Dame Press, 1986), p. 59.
10 Charles Fried, "Is Liberty Possible?" in *Liberty, Equality and the Law*, Sterling M. McMurrin (ed.) (Salt Lake City: University of Utah Press, 1987), p. 101.
11 Elizabeth Anderson, *Values in Ethics and Economics* (Cambridge, MA: Harvard University Press, 1993), p. 191.

8 Benchmarks and Moral Discernment

Conflicting Norms

The conflict among norms has been a constant refrain in the previous chapters. Two benchmarks can take us in different directions as we evaluate policies and policy options. There is no magic formula that provides a simple or easy resolution when making choices among competing values. This final chapter provides some suggestions about how to navigate among conflicting norms in the complex and complicated world of public policy making. The discussion that follows is based on three assumptions.

The first assumption is that the five benchmarks will often conflict with one another. There may be times when these norms are mutually reinforcing and complementary. We cannot assume, however, a congruence among the concerns embodied in these principles. There will be many occasions when governance decisions will require making a choice between competing benchmarks.

We get some clues about how to make moral decisions when faced with conflicting benchmarks in the work of W.D. Ross.[1] Emphasizing the complexity of moral life, Ross identified multiple prima facie duties which play a role in determining what ought to be done in any particular case. Any number of those prima facie obligations, which may even contradict one another, can apply in a single set of circumstances. One duty can be outweighed by another, with one of them carrying the most weight in a given situation. He considered these prima facie duties, in that the obligations are not absolute; we have a duty to obey one of them, unless that duty is outweighed by the obligation to follow another. This plurality of moral requirements creates multiple responsibilities that we can draw on to determine what we ought to do—all things considered.

The second assumption is that one particular norm does not *always* trump another. None of the benchmarks always takes precedence over all of the others, nor do any of them always yield to the others. The competition among principles is one in which weight is given to the moral force of each of them. This weight will vary from situation to situation with the result that a different norm will be the "winner" at different times. Policy decisions do not require the satisfaction of any one norm in every case at the expense of the other concerns. What is required is an analysis of specific contexts, rather than the imposition of solutions based on an a priori preeminence that has been granted on an ideological basis.

The third assumption is a more generalized form of the second. Not only is it the case that one of these benchmarks does not always override another, but in many individual cases one of them does not completely annul another in that specific instance. Each benchmark embodies moral values that are important. We would rarely want to ignore completely the interests that are served by any of the principles. There certainly have been occasions when the balance has been tipped heavily in one direction or another. For example, abrogation of prior commitments has been quickly accepted in times of war. Usually, however, when we are doing our weighing and balancing it is with an eye to finding optimal ways to incorporate something from all sets of values.

A feature of this in-the-situation balancing is the reality that assessments of governance options in light of the benchmarks often do not yield absolute answers. That is, the question of whether one particular option satisfies the requirements of a principle is not always a "yes" or a "no"—such as "Yes, this option is perfectly effective," or "No, this option fails all tests of fidelity." Many times the answer will be "to an extent." Real alternatives satisfy moral norms to a degree. And the more we move away from yes/no bimodal answers, the more complex the policy assessment process becomes.

What's Going On?

Disagreements about public policies are often rooted in disagreements about facts. Was the University of Michigan School of Law making admissions decisions based on quotas, or not? The answer to this question was determinative for many people when supporting or opposing the U.S. Supreme Court decision upholding affirmative action in the *Grutter* case. Did Saddam Hussein's Iraq possess weapons of mass destruction or not? Is being gay a matter of personal lifestyle choice or is it reflective of individual identity? Is "it" (the fetus in a woman's womb in the case of abortion; the embryo in a Petri dish in the case of stem cell research) a human life, or not? Where one comes out on "factual" questions such as these shapes the moral judgments that will be made about the appropriate policy response.

Before we ask the question "What ought we to do?" we should first ask "What is going on?" We can respond appropriately—in a way that fits a specific context—only if we know what that context is, if we understand the realities to which we are responding. Because we continually encounter new, unique situations, it is crucial to begin the decision making process by understanding the circumstances in which we must make our decisions. One aspect of understanding what is going on is the accumulation of pertinent data, obtaining accurate information about the existing state of affairs.

This collection of raw data is necessary. But developing an understanding of a current scene requires much more than that. We must distinguish important information from unimportant information. A reading of the situation and its meaning for assessing public policy entails insightful interpretation. We are required to draw inferences from the data, to make use of this information in imaginative ways, to develop a coherent view of realities that fits the facts together in meaningful ways.

Even though more is required, we should not give short shrift to the task of "merely" finding and understanding facts. The world is ever changing. Politicians and policy makers are often criticized for changing their prescriptions for resolving society's ills from one time to another. Because we encounter new, unique, dynamic conditions, however, "flip flopping" is not necessarily a bad thing. We *should* change our decisions and prescriptions as circumstances change. We should not be making policy based on static and outdated views of reality.

Finding out what's going on is one of the biggest problems facing us as we attempt to evaluate policy needs. All too often, people are making their decisions and basing their arguments on information that's just wrong, according to any credible news source. This is not an entirely new problem. Governmental secrecy and deception by "news makers" have long complicated the efforts of many citizens to get the facts in the service of evaluating public policies. This is why openness and honesty in government are so important, so that citizens and others who have an obligation to exercise their voice in the policy arena can do so responsibly. But the wide dispersal of sources of information, especially on the Internet, has created a new dimension to the problem, to the point that presidential campaigns now have to assign staffers to the task of constantly monitoring and correcting intentionally false statements about their candidates. One recent example is a report from the Pew Research Center that the percentage of Americans who think President Barack Obama is a Muslim increased from 11 percent to 18 percent between March 2009 and August 2010—a span of 16 months during which virtually every traditional news source reported that the rumor was not true.

Not only is agreement about what's going on in the present difficult to fashion, we can't even agree on the past. Consider, as an illustration, two book reviews of Jon Meacham's *American Gospel: God, the Founding Fathers, and the Making of a Nation*.[2] These two reviews, by reputable scholars, appeared side-by-side in the same journal and offered conflicting views. One reviewer labels this a "confused book" that offers a "historically inaccurate account" that "obscures and retards" an understanding of the history of religion and politics in the United States.[3] The other reviewer sees this as a "splendid book" which "makes available a great deal of historical information," providing an "insightful treatment" of the subject.[4] When mainline scholars have such dramatically different understandings of the realities of the past, one must almost despair of the prospect of developing any consensus about present reality. Further, if knowing present reality is difficult, projecting future reality is even more challenging. Yet, that kind of projecting is what is required to assess policies and especially proposed policies.

Understanding Benchmarks

We do not come to situations empty-headed. We bring with us the values and beliefs and moral principles that I'm calling benchmarks. I was first introduced to the use of "benchmarks" in the sense used in this book by James Sellers' *Public Ethics: American Morals and Manners*.[5] Sellers employed the image of the benchmark to distinguish one kind of norm from another, as a way of talking about "horizontal norms" (that he was embracing) while attempting to steer readers away from more traditional ways of thinking about "vertical norms." The traditional vertical norms were externally imposed, authoritative prescriptions of conduct that were relatively permanent. He used "benchmark" as a label for a different kind of norm, norms that are drawn from our common experience, and that are authoritative because they are recognized as what we need to cope with current problems and predicaments.

I use the term "benchmark" to distinguish my use of the concepts of benefit, effectiveness, fairness, fidelity and legitimacy from a use of principles that entails a rigid application of definite standards in an almost mechanistic way. A characterization of benchmarks can echo the kind of language Sellers used in talking about horizontal norms: these are ethical patterns, signposts, flexible models for conduct with a pragmatic bent to them. They are experimental and open to the unexpected. These characteristics call to mind Rawls' search for reflective equilibrium, in which general principles and particular judgments continually reinforce and refine one another through their interplay in specific cases. For many readers, this characterization may be uncomfortably off the mark from the fixed moral principles that are embodied in some ethical systems. A description of the traditional use of physical benchmarks may be helpful in explaining why I find them a useful analogy for the appropriation of moral values.

In the world of surveying, benchmarks were marks that surveyors cut in durable materials, such as rocks or walls, which were to be used as reference points in surveying lines to determine altitudes. Since these marks are used repeatedly over time, they need to be relatively stable points.[6] The interest in stability lies in the need for fixed points of reference to which surveyors and engineers can return for surveying, engineering, mapping, land use planning, and scientific projects. It is understood, however, that this stability is relative; the goal is for a high degree of accuracy, not absolute accuracy. A number of factors come into play that affect the degree of precision and stability that is feasible, or even the amount of precision that is desired or required. For some projects, it is uneconomical to spend the time and money necessary to set higher quality benchmarks.

Even when a high degree of precision and stability is desired, the only basis for appraising benchmark stability is the Earth's crust, and that crust is in constant motion. For those of us who feel solid ground under our feet, it is useful to understand that the movement of benchmarks can be likened by geologists to the movement of a float bobbing up and down on the surface of the ocean—a float whose position is affected not only by waves and swells but also by the coming and going of the tides. Factors that affect the stability of benchmarks on dry land include subsurface activities (including crustal motion, gradual subsidence over caverns, more abrupt movement over sink holes, and subsidence caused by the pumping of oil or water), and on- or near-surface activities such as frost heave; shrinking and swelling of soil and rock; slope instability; erosion; and soil expansion, contraction and consolidation. The gravitational effects of the sun and moon exert influences on land masses, creating a phenomenon known as "Earth tides." And there is always the possibility of human interference: vandalism, tampering by souvenir hunters, or total destruction caused by earth-moving equipment.

The main points I want to take away from the geological benchmarks analogy are: (1) they provide critically important points of reference; (2) they provide us with approximations which orient our thinking and action; (3) they evolve over time; and (4) judgment is required to develop and use these standards appropriately. First, these are critically important points of reference. The five ethical benchmarks provide meaningful guidance. They specify clusters of values that should orient our thinking. They identify factors which should be taken into account, which must be addressed in any adequate assessment of public policy. These are bedrock principles that we bring with us into each situation.

Second, these benchmarks are approximations. I know that I am revealing my age by saying that reading about benchmarks reminded me of the days of my youth when we used slide rules to solve the complex mathematical equations that are solved with much more precision these days by calculators. As for moral benchmarks, even if we knew with precision exactly what they would require of us in a given set of circumstances, I have no expectation that any of them, much less all of them, would be perfectly and fully maximized by any real-world public policy. At the very least, it appears that the degree to which we can approach the complete satisfaction of any benchmark is likely to be limited by the effort to simultaneously satisfy others.

Third, surveying benchmarks do change their relationship to the ground; the ground literally shifts beneath them. In the case of ethical benchmarks, these are bedrock principles, but the bedrock does change. Our world changes, and we are continually learning more about our world. The meaning that our community ascribes to fairness or fidelity, for example, will be altered as we move from one historical context to another. Finally, as with geological benchmarks, skilled judgment is required to make use of ethical benchmarks. With our societal commitment that respects and protects individual liberty and freedom of conscience, we are not surprised that different people come to different conclusions about matters of ethics and public policy—in fact, we expect it. Even within a particular historical context, these norms do not have a single, rigid, static meaning. No one understanding of fairness (such as equal shares, or the ability to pay) is appropriate in all cases. No one criterion of legitimacy is the necessary and sufficient justification for government action in all cases. Measurement of benefit is not confined to a single economic method. We should not succumb to the "foolish consistency" that Emerson attributed to little minds. Further, there is no fixed relation among the various norms. The approach taken in this book is to avoid giving preeminence, a fixed priority, to one over another. That being the case, more needs to be said about an approach to moral decision making which is nuanced in this way, which is more than logical deduction from first principles.

Moral Discernment

Policy issues are complicated because we do not operate with a single preeminent principle. We do not have a single guiding star that directs us to the right answers if we just reason long enough and carefully enough. Rather, we adhere to a multitude of contending and conflicting values in our policy choices. Our moral task is not to deliberate toward a particular one-trumps-all end, or from a particular one-trumps-all rule. Rather our task is to navigate among an immense jumble of benchmarks, beliefs, ideals, goals, and values, and to find the paths that provide the best fit in our ever-changing environment. We are called to be morally discerning.

Discernment resides at the core of making moral judgments. Discernment is one of those words that are so powerful that they evade adequate definition. The process begins with a perceptive reading of a situation, grasping what is at stake in the moment and recognizing what binds this situation to, and distinguishes it from, other situations. It entails a deep reading of the facts and relationships that constitute the encountered reality. A moral sensitivity identifies the values and moral principles that bear on the choices to be made, and breathes meaning into those generalizations for the task at hand. Excellence in moral discernment requires perceptivity, discrimination, subtlety, sensitivity and clarity. It is "impossible to program, and difficult to describe."[7]

We apply the label "discerning" to persons who seem to be more perceptive, wiser, more discriminating in their judging. These persons exemplify a particular acuity in their perception or observation; they locate details that others miss, with an unusual capacity to isolate significant details, and to notice subtleties. They have a way of getting at salient characteristics, with an eye for pertinent features. Just as the discerning literary critic helps the reader "see" things in the literature that she might not see on her own, a discerning moral analysis is more sensitive to nuances, to details and their suggestive meanings.

The discerning process I have in mind embraces a pluralism of considerations, with no absolute allegiance given to any single principle. It rejects approaches such as those that propose that benefit should always trump fairness and justice,[8] or that liberty should be granted supremacy over equality and community.[9] A summary of traits and activities that are embodied in discernment is more focused on process than on outcomes: penetrating beneath the surface to discover subtle nuances and complexities; teasing out suggestive meanings; distilling pertinence, relevance and salience; perceiving relationships and drawing inferences; an empathetic appreciation of needs and aspirations; an imaginative capacity to figure out how it all fits together. We seek a coherence that moves us away from confusion and inconsistency.

In the end, we know the adequacy of a morally discerning process by its fruits. Such a process will provide policies that we find compelling, powerful and persuasive—policies that solve problems and address needs in satisfactory ways. We are not anchorless in making these judgments. We should be concerned that benefits are provided (or harms avoided), that those benefits are provided and harms avoided in an effective way, that burdens and benefits are distributed fairly, and that the policies that serve these concerns are implemented in a manner that is respectful of persons.

Embracing Humility

We should approach the task of assessing public policy with humility. Carol Weiss has argued that public policy positions are the results of three sets of forces: information, ideologies and interests.[10] Each of us has good reason to be humble about our own footing on all three scores. First, policy positions are based on information, a descriptive understanding of current circumstances, the facts. But what we know is partial and mediated through other sources. We can have little first-hand observation of the total world that public policies are designed to address, and competing sources of information provide enough conflicting data that we know that we never know the entire story. Weiss chooses to use the term information rather than knowledge, because "knowledge" communicates a sense of accuracy, rightness, and validity—and she wants to take cognizance of the partial, biased and invalid understandings that influence the forming of policy decisions.

The key role that information plays in policy making was highlighted by the leaking in November of 2009 of thousands of emails and other documents from the University of East Anglia's Climate Research Unit. The publication of these materials prompted a firestorm of questions, accusations and counter-accusations. The energy expended on analyzing and re-analyzing the documents demonstrates the recognition by parties on all sides of this controversy that valid, reliable information is critical for proper decision making. If the information that flowed from this source was questionable, then so were the policies that were based on this information.

Despite our best efforts, we will inevitably find ourselves in the position accurately described by Secretary of Defense Donald Rumsfeld when he observed that we don't even know what we don't know. We will make policy judgments based on information that is fragmentary, uncertain, contested, fluid, and open to radically different interpretations—even by good-faith interpreters. That reality alone should be enough to introduce more than a touch of humility into our policy proclamations.

A second major influence on the formation of policy positions is ideology. For Weiss this encompasses philosophy, principles, political orientation—at the core, we're talking about moral values. These may be carefully constructed and internally consistent systems, or they may be haphazard collections of ideas put together in a piecemeal way. Either way, they constitute a normative orientation that provides a basis for position taking. Some individuals hold their normative positions with what appears to be absolute certitude, but history is full of moral positions that were once held with a similar certainty and that are now completely discredited. There will be partisans on all sides of most issues who appear to be ignorant, or just greedily pursuing their own interests. However, we cannot help but notice that there are also people on all sides of debates who are intelligent, well-informed, well-meaning, and making good faith efforts to support what is truly best for the community. We've heard the countless stories of individuals who have moved from strongly believing one position to strongly believing the opposite position. New information changes ideology. American politicians who were committed segregationists later reversed course and apologized for their previous beliefs. Many economists converted from being monetarists to being supporters of deficit spending when they saw monetary policy alone failing to deliver us from the Great Recession. Such examples should give us some pause when reflecting on the certainty with which we want to push our ideological convictions in the formation of policy that governs a diverse community.

Weiss defines interests, the third basis for policy positions, in terms of self-interest. Such self-interests include those of taxpayers who want to pay lower taxes, groups of beneficiaries who want to maintain or increase their benefits, consumers who want a low rate of inflation—as well as legislators who want to get re-elected and bureaucrats who want to expand their bureaus and advance their own careers. Only the saints among us deliberate about policies in ways that are totally devoid of self-interest. There is a lot of truth in the old bromide about taking policy positions, that where you stand depends on where you sit. Knowing this, we should have enough humility about our own positions to turn our sharpest critical analysis on ourselves.

The role self-interest plays in our thinking is often unconscious. We may be convinced that our choices are based on knowledge and values, when in fact our information and ideologies are themselves influenced by our interests. This possibility reflects the final complicating point that Weiss makes:

the three factors of information, ideology and interests are constantly interacting with each other, shaping and re-shaping the roles they play in our decision making. There is so little that we know; there is so little certainty we can have about our choices. We should approach policy decision making with a humility that is grounded in an acknowledgement of our finitude. But there must be another part of the message: we cannot be paralyzed, we cannot fail to act when we have the possibility of improving the lives of so many people. Thus, a dose of humility must be balanced with doses of compassion for those whom government serves and of passion to make a difference where we can.

Passion and Compassion

Through the course of this book, we've encountered many factors that could push us into a paralysis, which in turn leaves the status quo intact. I've suggested that many policy decisions are close calls, with important, well-reasoned arguments being made on opposing sides. Policy choices invariably entail tradeoffs, with many them coming down to 51–49 calls. Our predictions about what will result from new policies are always uncertain. "Better the devil you know" is an often-expressed view that counsels avoidance of the risk that comes with making any change. The endowment effect identifies another pull toward the status quo, as we typically over-value what we have or under-value what we might obtain in the future. We tend to judge ourselves and others more harshly on sins of commission than sins of omission. The breadth and depth of social problems that could be addressed are mind-numbing, and it is easier to generate compassion for those close to us, such as family, friends and neighbors, than it is for those who comprise the "faceless masses." Finally, the humility I have just advocated in our adoption of policy positions is not exactly a call to storm the barricades.

Nevertheless, we must find the moral courage and the political will to act. Some cases are close, but even those cases make a difference, sometimes a powerful difference, in the lives of those who are affected. The tenor of my suggestion here has echoes of Martin Luther's letter to Philip Melancthon when he wrote, "Be a sinner and sin boldly. . . . As long as we are here we have to sin." As long as we are in this world, we have to make decisions based on uncertain premises and knowledge, with unknown results in store. Mistakes will be made. That is a reality of the human condition. And it is certainly a reality of policy making. But we cannot allow the perfect to become the enemy of the good, and lapse into inaction.

A compassion for those affected by government policy can produce a passion that motivates us to act. It is easy to act out of compassion for a person we see suffering, or one in need who is close to us. That kind of personal compassion comes to us more naturally than does a statistical compassion—a caring for those whom we encounter only in statistics in policy projections and analysis. Efforts to put ourselves in the shoes of those distant neighbors can influence policy decisions. Creating these connections often requires going an extra mile in extending our analysis of options.

In 2008, the Metropolitan Transit Authority budget in Nashville, Tennessee, was in deficit. The problem could be easily solved by terminating seven bus routes. But the city did not take the easy path. The city did not approach the problem as a matter of mathematical computations involving variables such as the number of riders, fares per line, and cost per rider to run each line. There were concerns about the effects on the lives of the people who actually relied on that transportation, especially workers who had to get to work every day, and students who had no alternative ways to get to a magnet school. There were concerns that shrinking the bus system would lessen its viability, and would certainly set back efforts to promote mass transit and improve the environment. During the public discussion of the problem, the Brookings Institution published a study which ranked Nashville as the sixth worst city among the country's 100 largest metropolitan areas in carbon emissions—due in significant part to dependence on cars over mass transit. Ultimately, the city government expanded the field of play and shifted funds from another part of the city's budget. The number of bus routes being eliminated was reduced, and a few years later the bus system was being expanded.

The goal in making decisions about bus lines and balanced budgets should not be just to solve a puzzle, balancing the equations, to produce the kind of satisfaction one gets from solving the puzzle in a Sudoku box. Compassion forces us to think outside of this particular box—to not only look at equations within it, but to also look at the relative value of dollars spent elsewhere in the budget; the level of service and subsidy that is appropriate to serve the community's needs; the proper level of taxation; the boarder implications for increasing or cutting service for the community beyond the current passengers. A compassionate caring about the impacts on the lives of people forces a broader look. Raising taxes cannot be and should not always be the answer, because the breadth of our compassion should also encompass those who are burdened by those levies.

Compassion can also provide a sharpening of one's vision. When problems are kept at arm's length, it is easy to satisfy our intellectual curiosity and be content with a conclusion that the choice is a difficult one. But, if one is committed to coming to a decision, if embarking on a course of action is mandated by one's caring about those in need, then the inquiry is more likely to be pushed farther. We should be driven by a commitment to figure out the best thing to do under the circumstances. Competing and conflicting claims should not be just noted, but weighed, evaluated and assessed—until eventually priorities are aligned in a way that leads to action. Assessing policy alternatives should take us beyond idle curiosity, and flaccid musings. We should be compelled to think longer and deeper and harder and more broadly when something important is at stake. This stretching of our analytical capacities and imagination is not only more challenging, it is more rewarding . . . when we get it right.

Living in Community

Finally, we need an approach to public discourse about policy making that recognizes that we live in community, and that strengthens the bonds of community. The moral question in public policy making is not so much what should *I* do, but what should *we* do. We are making decisions about the best course of action for our community, determining the appropriate actions the government should take on behalf of all of us. Further, we make these judgments as members of a community. Acknowledging that we live in community engenders the humility that we should bring to the governing process. We know that none of us, acting alone, can create the world we want. And we know that our thoughts and beliefs have been created in community. We come to our decisions about policy matters as persons who have grown up in specific traditions and who live in the midst of loyalties to other persons and to shared causes. Thus, it is not just the subject of our inquiry that is social, but the very process of our inquiring is social through and through.

The process of governing should be a way that we keep faith with each other. When the government acts, it is we who act through that institution. In the broadest sense, government should be an instrument used by "we the people." We do not very often, of course, experience government action that way. We think and talk about government as "it" rather than "we." We identify those who control policy as "them" rather than "us." It is difficult to think of the community as a "we" when so much of the body that participates in the political process has been fragmented into interest groups. We are told that there is not *a* "public interest" but only a collection of individual and group interests, competing with one another.

The litany of problems is a familiar one. "Special interests" have outsized influence. Big money buys access, distorts public discussions, controls elections, and unduly affects policy makers. Interest groups are more interested in winning in their competition with other groups than they are in fashioning sound policy. Rancor and discord dominate the media because that's what boosts ratings. Too many politicians are focused on re-election and amassing power to advance their own careers. The consequence of all these factors seems to be an adversarial environment in which crass partisanship crowds out good-faith efforts to make policy that truly serves the public. Too much of the rhetoric we hear is designed to trump, polarize, disenfranchise or discredit others—rather than seeking convergence as we make policy together.

We know that we are not going to reach unanimous consent on some kind of ideal moral judgment. Further, we cannot expect—and we don't want—people to give up on what they care about. We cannot expect and do not want people to quit fighting for what they believe is right. Efforts to improve the policy making climate should not be about surrendering one's own causes and subsuming one's values to those of others. Rather the focus has to be about how we proceed, how we govern our common lives given these differences. Our discussions should not be about crushing an opponent, but looking for value in the other, based in a continuing openness to learn. Political leaders, in fact all citizens, should be working to foster a process that promotes the reconstruction of an understanding of the public interest. Reaching consensus agreements on the *substance* of policies in many areas of our common life will be rare. Progress on reaching agreement about *processes* that are in the public interest should be more attainable.

The starting point is community. We can imagine a model for how a community governs itself. In this ideal model, we would assess problems and reach our conclusions in conversation with one another. We would present our arguments, and listen to the arguments of others, before judgments are made. A good rule of thumb is to listen to others as you would want them to listen to you. After decisions are made, we all offer reasons for those decisions as the conversation continues the processes of review, reassessment and revision. These community conversations do not begin *de novo*. Values and principles that have been helpful in the past in navigating challenges are called upon, perhaps rearranged, and used to provide illumination for the present community. Moral discernment takes place in continuity with the past. We learn from previous successes and failures, informed and directed by the past without being determined by it. A notion of community solidarity affects our public discourse about policy. These discussions should be carried out in ways that are respectful of others in the community. At a minimum, this means that we do not engage in *ad hominem* arguments. We don't intentionally distort the facts. We assume that we can always benefit from new information, from hearing new perspectives.

Of course, these statements are little more than platitudes, to which most parties would be willing to pay lip service. A more substantial contribution to assessing the way a community governs itself is an examination of the kinds of reasons that are advanced in our public discourse. John Rawls has argued that policy decisions in a liberal democracy such as the United States should be based on "public reason"—reasons that are publicly accessible and that "all citizens can reasonably be expected to endorse in the light of their common human reason."[11] The idea is that our public conversations should be conducted solely in terms of political values that all citizens can be reasonably be expected to accept. Amy Gutmann and Dennis Thompson have developed a concept of deliberative democracy, in which "reciprocity" regulates the public reasons that citizens should use to justify their claims to one another. According to this concept, you make your claims on terms that I can accept in principle, and I make my claims on terms that you can accept in principle. Gutmann and Thompson describe the limits their approach places on our public discourse as follows: "When citizens make moral claims in a deliberative democracy, they appeal to reasons or principles that can be shared by fellow citizens who are similarly motivated." In this context, those who are "similarly motivated" are those who are willing to press their public claims in terms that are "accessible to their fellow citizens."[12]

These approaches offer publicly accessible reasons as the basis for attempts to resolve disputes. Restricting moral claims to those that are based on reasons that are accessible to all citizens limits the nature and scope of disagreement. Achieving agreement on such limitations would appear to increase civility in our pubic exchanges and lead to more productive outcomes in reaching agreement on policy decisions. However, there is much to be said about deciding which reasons are publicly accessible, and employing this distinction may not actually advance the desirable goals of civility and productive results.

A key question is whether a reciprocity standard would exclude religious reasons from a deliberative democracy process. Remember that the inquiry is not about the types of reasons that we should all agree to adopt, but just the reasons that citizens could legitimately proffer in the public debate. Put simply, the question is whether there is a place for religious beliefs in the public square. If religious claims are deemed, by their very nature, to be inaccessible to one's fellow citizens, then this approach to developing a community-building, community-binding deliberative process based on mutual respect would exclude many members of the community—or at least would exclude core values held by many members of the community.

Human reason is the basis used by both Rawls, and Gutmann and Thompson for identifying publicly accessible principles. But a significant number of observers who use this standard of reasonableness find some religious beliefs to be inaccessible to the public. The cause of civility and mutual respect is hardly served by telling a large number of our citizens that their beliefs and values are not even worthy of consideration in a deliberative policy making process. We should avoid closing our minds to those whose minds we think are closed. It seems that the reciprocity criteria effort to establish a common basis for resolving substantive disputes on policy matters succeeds only in creating new disputes about what that common basis should be.

No major policy decision is made based on a single reason. Little is lost and much is gained if one type of argument that is welcomed in the public sphere, among many others in the cacophony of public voices, is a religious one. Religious beliefs will not appeal to all. Still, the ideals of mutuality and reciprocity are better served if we make room in our public discourse for all beliefs and perspectives, not just those that meet some views of what human reason allows. I suggest a different dividing line that we can establish between arguments that are welcomed in the public square and those that we consider to be beyond the pale.

We can make an important distinction in our public discourse between argumentation that strengthens our public debate and argumentation that weakens it. Reasons can be offered in ways that advance the conversation or that subvert it. Some proclamations invite communal deliberation and some shut it down. It is true that some religiously-grounded arguments do stop the conversation, but it doesn't have to be that way. Governor Mike Huckabee has espoused an alternative approach: "I'm a conservative, but I'm not mad at anybody about it. I've learned that you don't have to give up your own convictions. But you do need to be willing to have an open mind, spirit and heart toward people who are completely different from you."

Religious rhetoric is not the only kind of argumentation that can play a destructive role in our community. Those without a religious bone in their bodies can diminish the prospect for meaningful communication through intolerance, intimidation and the demonization of opponents. The organized disruption of public health care forums around the country in August of 2009 was designed to sabotage informed public discourse, and these subversive efforts did not appear to have an explicitly-religious basis to them. If we are establishing preconditions for admission to the public debate on policy, the precondition should be respect for the community, for the public forum, for the deliberative process of which one wants to be a part.

This approach allows religiously-based reasons, and other forms of argument that might be considered "unreasonable," into the mix—to be weighed and assessed by those involved in the process. Acknowledging a legitimate place for such arguments in the public sphere does not require a judgment that such types of reasons are necessary or sufficient to policy assessment. Indeed, for some who do not share those perspectives, the weight given to those arguments may be zero. But even those who personally give no weight to a particular religious argument should welcome the contributions of all citizens as a part of a community-building, community-affirming process.

Through participation in our common moral deliberation, capacities to make discerning judgments can be deepened, broadened and extended. We can evaluate the function of a public policy decision making process by whether it has enhanced the community's discourse or destroyed it. Arguments that enhance our community discourse are those that provide new information, offer a different perspective, or introduce competing values that have been ignored. Arguments that destroy that discourse are those that launch *ad hominem* attacks, coerce through intimidation, or perhaps most insidiously substitute falsehoods and distortions for honesty and accuracy. The question is whether we as a community have grown in our public discourse or shrunk, whether we have expanded our capacities to make moral assessments or crippled them.

Returning to our beginning question—what should we do?—the deliberative process itself is an answer. In this respect public moral discourse resembles Madison's view of the Constitution and the political efficacy of public argument itself: a view that "the trip was the true destination."[13]

The purpose of a public moral deliberative process is to produce policies that are reflective of our societal values. The desirable outcomes are policies that protect our liberties, enhance our welfare, and that are fair to and respectful of every member of our community. And, as we have seen, the debates about precisely what those values require in ever-changing landscapes appear to be endless. In the end, the most important result coming out of our communal moral assessment of public policy may well be a strengthening of that deliberative process itself.

Notes

1 See especially W.D. Ross, *The Right and the Good* (Oxford: Oxford University Press, 1930. Reprinted with an introduction by Philip Stratton-Lake, 2002.)
2 Jon Meacham, *American Gospel: God, the Founding Fathers, and the Making of a Nation* (New York: Random House, 2006).
3 Garrett Ward Shelton, book review, *Journal of Church and State*, vol. 50, no. 1 (Winter 2008), pp. 143–5.
4 Paul Simmons, book review, *Journal of Church and State*, vol. 50, no. 1 (Winter 2008), pp. 145–7.
5 James Sellers, *Public Ethics: American Morals and Manners* (New York: Harper & Row, 1970).
6 Much of the discussion of bench marks here is drawn from Richard P. Floyd, "Geodetic Bench Marks," NOAA Manual NOS NGS 1 (Washington: U.S. Government Printing Office), September 1978.
7 James M. Gustafson, *Moral Discernment in the Christian Life: Essays in Theological Ethics*, Theo A. Boer and Paul I. Capetz, eds. (Louisville, KY: Westminster John Knox Press, 2007), pp. 25–40. Many of the characterizations of the elements of moral discernment in this text draw on Gustafson's insightful discussion.
8 Louis Kaplow and Steven Shavell, *Fairness Versus Welfare* (Cambridge, MA: Harvard University Press, 2002).
9 Charles Fried, *Modern Liberty and the Limits of Government* (New York: W.W. Norton Co., 2007).
10 Carol H. Weiss, "Ideology, Interests and Information: The Basis of Policy Positions," in *Ethics, the Social Sciences and Policy Analysis*, Daniel Callahan and Bruce Jennings, eds. (New York: Plenum Press, 1983), pp. 213–45.
11 John Rawls, *Political Liberalism* (New York: Columbia University Press, 1993), p. 140; see also pp. 212–54.
12 Amy Gutmann and Dennis Thompson, *Democracy and Disagreement* (Cambridge, MA: Harvard University Press, 1996), p. 55.
13 Joseph J. Ellis, *American Creation: Triumphs and Tragedies at the Founding of the Republic* (New York: Alfred A. Knopf, 2007), p. 124.

Benediction

The prayer below was offered by my friend Jena Lee Nardella at the Democratic National Convention on September 4, 2012.

God, I stand before You and ask that the words of my mouth and the meditations of my heart be pleasing unto You.

I pray for our President, Barack Obama. May he know Your presence, oh God, as he continues to serve as a leader of this nation, as a husband to Michelle, and as father to his daughters. Help him to seek justice, love mercy and walk humbly with you.

I pray as well for Governor Mitt Romney. May he know Your presence, oh God, as he continues to serve as a leader, as a husband to Ann, and as a father to his sons and their families. Help him to see justice, love mercy and walk humbly with you.

I pray for our country in the next nine weeks leading up to this election—for those of us meeting here and for our fellow citizens who met last week. May we make our children proud of how we conduct ourselves. We know our human tendencies toward finger-pointing and frivolousness. Our better selves want this race to be honest and edifing rather than fabricated and self-serving.

Give us, oh Lord, humility to listen to our sisters and brothers across the political spectrum, because your kingdom is not divided into Red States and Blue States. Equip us with moral imagination to have real discourse. Knit us, of God, as one country even as we wrestle over the complexity of how we ought to live and govern. Give us gratitude for our right to dissent and disagree. For we know that we are bound up in one another and have been given the tremendous opportunity to extend humanity and grace when others voice their deeply held convictions even when they differ from our own.

And give us wisdom, God, to discover honest solutions for we know it will take all of us to care for the widow and the orphan, the sick and the lonely, the downtrodden and the unemployed, the prisoner and the homeless, the stranger and the enemy, the thirsty and the powerless. In rural Africa, I am witness to thousands of HIV positive mothers, fathers and children who are alive today because Democrats and Republicans put justice and mercy above partisanship. Help us keep that perspective even as we debate one another.

God, I thank you for the saving grace of Jesus and for the saints who have humbly gone before us. I thank you for the words of St. Francis of Assisi whose prayer I carry with me both in my home in East Nashville and in my work across rural Africa.

As we enter this election season, I pray St. Francis' words for us all.

Lord, make us instruments of your peace. Where there is hatred, let us sow love; where there is injury, pardon; where there is discord, union; where there is doubt, faith; where there is despair, hope; where there is darkness, light; and where there is sadness, joy.

Grant that we may not so much seek to be consoled as to console; to be understood as to understand; to be loved as to love. For it is giving that we receive; it is in pardoning that we are pardoned; and it is dying that we are born to eternal life. Amen.

Sources Cited

Anderson, Elizabeth. *Value in Ethics and Economics*. Cambridge, MA: Harvard University Press, 1993.

Beauchamp, Tom L., and Childress, James. *Principles of Biomedical Ethics*, 7th ed. New York: Oxford University Press, 2012.

Breyer, Stephen. *Breaking the Vicious Circle*. Cambridge, MA: Harvard University Press, 1993.

Califano, Joseph A., Jr. *Governing America: An Insider's Report from the White House and the Cabinet*. New York: Simon and Schuster, 2007.

Carruthers, Peter. *The Animals Issue: Moral Theory in Practice*. Cambridge: Cambridge University Press, 1992.

Carter, Jimmy. *Our Endangered Values: America's Moral Crisis*. New York: Simon and Schuster, 2005.

Corrosion Proof Fittings v. Environmental Protection Agency, 947 F.2d 1201 (5th Cir. 1991)

Deigh, John. *An Introduction to Ethics*. Cambridge: Cambridge University Press, 2010.

Devlin, Patrick. *The Enforcement of Morals*. London: Oxford University Press, 1965.

Douthat, Ross. "War, What Is It Good For?" *The New York Times*, September 1, 2013.

Ellis, Joseph J. *American Creation: Triumphs and Tragedies at the Founding of the Republic*. New York: Alfred A. Knopf, 2007.

Feinberg, Joel. *Offense to Others*. New York: Oxford University Press, 1985.

Foley, Elizabeth Price. *Liberty for All: Reclaiming Individual Privacy in a New Era of Morality*. New Haven: Yale University Press, 1969.

Floyd, Richard P. "Geodetic Bench Marks." NOAA Manual NOS NGS 1. Washington: Government Printing Office, 1978.

Frankena, William K. *Ethics*, 2nd ed. Englewood Cliffs, NJ: Prentice-Hall, 1973.

Fried, Charles. "Is Liberty Possible?" In *Liberty, Equality and the Law*, edited by Sterling M. McMurrin, 91–135. Salt Lake City, UT: University of Utah Press, 1987.

———. *Modern Liberty and the Limits of Government*. New York: W.W. Norton & Co., 2007.

Fuller, Lon L. *The Morality of Law*, rev. ed. New Haven: Yale University Press, 1969.

Geertz, Clifford. *The Interpretation of Cultures*. New York: Basic Books, 1973.

George, Robert P. *Making Men Moral: Civil Liberties and Public Morality*. Oxford: Clarendon Press, 1993.

Gilligan, Carol. "Remapping the Moral Domain: New Images of Self in the Relationship." In *Mapping the Moral Domain*, edited by Carol Gilligan, Janie Victoria Ward and Jill McLean Taylor, 3–19. Cambridge, MA: Harvard University Press, 1988.

Gleick, James. *Chaos: Making a New Science*. New York: Viking Press, 1987.

Gustafson, James M. *Moral Discernment in the Christian Life: Essays in Theological Ethics, edited by Theo A. Boer and Paul I. Capetz*. Louisville, KY: Westminster John Knox Press, 2007.

Gutmann, Amy, and Thompson, Dennis. *Democracy and Disagreement*. Cambridge, MA: Harvard University Press, 1993.

———. *Ethics and Politics: Cases and Comments*, 4th ed. Belmont, CA: Thomson Wadsworth, 2006.

———. "Moral Conflict and Political Consensus." *Ethics* 101 (1990) 64–88.

Hart, H.L.A. *Law, Liberty and Morality*. Stanford, CA: Stanford University Press, 1963.

Held, Virginia. *The Ethics of Care: Personal, Political and Global*. New York: Oxford University Press, 2006.

Hicks, John R. "The Foundation of Welfare Economics." *Economic Journal* 49 (1939) 697–712.

Jack, Rand, and Jack, Dana Crowley. *Moral Vision and Professional Decisions: The Changing Values of Women and Men Lawyers*. Cambridge, MA: Harvard University Press, 1989.

Jonsen, Albert R., and Toulmin, Stephen. *The Abuse of Casuistry: A History of Moral Reasoning*. Berkeley, CA: University of California Press, 1988.

Kaldor, Nicholas. "Welfare Propositions of Economics and Interpersonal Comparisons of Utility." *Economic Journal* 49 (1939) 549–52.

Kaplow, Louis, and Shavell. *Fairness Versus Welfare*. Cambridge, MA: Harvard University Press, 2002.

Kelo v. City of New London, 545 U.S. 469 (2005).

King, Martin Luther, Jr. *Why We Can't Wait*. New York: Harper & Row, 1963.

Knetsch, Jack L. "Policy Analysis and Design with Losses Valued More that Gains and Varying Rates of Time Preferences." In *Judgments, Decisions and Public Policy*, edited by Rajeer Gowand and Jeffrey C. Fox, 91–115. Cambridge: Cambridge University Press, 2002.

Lawrence, William W. *Modern Science and Human Values*. New York: Oxford University Press, 1985.

Main, Carla T. *Bulldozed: "Kelo," Eminent Domain, and the American Lust for Land*. New York: Encounter Books, 2007.

McCarthy, Cormac. *The Crossing*. New York: Alfred A. Knopf, 1994.

Meacham Jon. *American Gospel: God, the Founding Fathers, and the Making of the Nation*. New York: Random House, 2006.

Mill, John Stuart. *On Liberty*. Chicago: Henry Regnery Co., 1859 (repr., Mineola, NY: Dover Publications, 2002).

Mooney, Christopher F. *Public Virtue: Law and the Social Character of Religion*. Notre Dame, IN: University of Notre Dame Press, 1986.

Murray, James. "Understanding Law as Metaphor." *The Journal of Legal Education* 34 (1984) 714–30.

Niebuhr, H. Richard. *The Responsible Self: An Essay in Christian Moral Philosophy.* New York: Harper and Row, 1963.

Nozick, Robert. *Anarchy, State and Utopia.* New York: Basic Books, 1974.

O'Hare, Michael, and Sanderson, Debra. "Facility Siting and Compensation: Lessons from the Massachusetts Experience." *Journal of Policy Analysis and Management* 12 (1993) 364–76.

Passel, Peter. "Disputed New Role for Polls: Putting a Price Tag on Nature" *The New York Times*, September 6, 1993.

Portney, Paul R. "Trouble in Happyville," *Journal of Policy Analysis and Management* 11 (1992) 131–2.

Rawls, John. *A Theory of Justice.* Cambridge, MA: Harvard University Press, 1974.

——. *Political Liberalism.* New York: Columbia University Press, 1993.

Regan, Tom. *The Case for Animal Rights.* London: Routledge, 1984.

Ross, W.D. *The Right and the Good.* Oxford: Oxford University Press, 1930.

Sagoff, Mark. *The Economy of the Earth: Philosophy, Law and the Environment,* 2nd ed. Cambridge: Cambridge University Press, 2008.

Sandel, Michael J. *Public Philosophy: Essays on Morality in Politics.* Cambridge, MA: Harvard University Press, 2005.

——. *What Money Can't Buy: The Moral Limits of Markets.* New York: Farrar, Strauss and Giroux, 2012.

Schmidt, Milton O., and Rayner, William Horace. *Fundamentals of Surveying,* 2nd ed. New York: Van Nostrand Co., 1978.

Sellers, James. *Public Ethics: American Morals and Manners.* New York: Harper & Row, 1970.

Shelton, Garrett Ward. Review of *American Gospel: God, the Founding Fathers, and the Making of a Nation,* by Jon Meacham. *Journal of Church and State* 50 (2008) 143–5.

Simmons, Paul. Review of *American Gospel: God, the Founding Fathers, and the Making of a Nation,* by Jon Meacham. *Journal of Church and State* 50 (2008) 145–7.

Singer, Peter. *Animal Rights: The Definitive Classic of the Animal Movement.* New York: HarperCollins, 2009.

Starhawk. *The Fifth Sacred Thing.* New York: Bantam Books, 1994.

Sunstein, Cass R. "Preferences and Politics," *Philosophy and Public Affairs* 20 (1991) 3–34.

Thompson, Dennis F. *Political Ethics and Public Office.* Cambridge, MA: Harvard University Press, 1987.

"Three Mile Island Accident." Fact Sheet of the Office of Public Affairs, United States Nuclear Regulatory Commission. (www.nrc.gov/reading-rm/doc-collections/fact-sheets/3mile-isle.html)(last updated February 11, 2013).

Trumbull, William N. "Reply to Whittington and MacRae," *Journal of Policy Analysis and Management* 9 (1990) 558–60.

—— "Who Has Standing in Cost-Benefit Analysis?" *Journal of Policy Analysis and Management* 9 (1990) 201–18.

Viscusi, W. Kip, and Aldy, Joseph E. "The Value of a Statistical Life: A Critical Review of Market Estimates Throughout the World." *The Journal of Risk and Uncertainty* 27 (2003) 5–76.

Weimer, David L., and Vining, Aidan R. *Policy Analysis: Concepts and Practice,* 4th ed. Upper Saddle River, NJ: Prentice-Hall, 2005.

Weiss, Carol H. "Ideology, Interests and Information: The Basis of Policy Positions." In *Ethics, the Social Sciences and Policy Analysis*. Edited by Daniel Callahan and Bruce Jennings. New York: Plenum Press, 1983, 213–45.

West, Henry R. *An Introduction to Mill's Utilitarian Ethics*. Cambridge: Cambridge University Press, 2004.

Whittington, Dale, and MacRae, Duncan, Jr. "Comment: Judgments about Who Has Standing in Cost-Benefit Analysis," *Journal of Policy Analysis and Management* 9 (1990) 536–47.

Wolfe, Christopher. "Public Morality and the Modern Supreme Court." *American Journal of Jurisprudence* 45 (2000) 65–92.

Index

abortion 19, 27, 107, 112–13, 130
achievement, to each based on 80
affective dimensions and connections 24, 25, 27
affirmative action 81, 85, 94–5, 130
age and fairness 80, 85
AIDS and HIV 52, 62
Alaska, *Exxon Valdez* disaster 46
alcohol: chronic overuse and liver transplantation 84; prohibition 112
Aldy, Joseph 46
American Smelting and Refining Company (ASARCO) 66–7
Anderson, Elizabeth 46
animal experimentation and well-being 39–40
anti-discrimination law 84–5, 93
arsenic and copper smelting 66–7
ASARCO (American Smelting and Refining Company) 66–7
asbestos 60
aspirations 2, 63, 93, 94, 110, 124
attributes, individual 85–6
autonomy 44, 87, 88, 89, 90, 91, 92, 95, 121

behavior (individual/personal) 84, 85, 86; offensive/criminal/unlawful 38, 116, 125
behavioral economics 75–8
benchmarks 4, 5, 17–23, 129–43; preview of the five types 28–30; understanding 132–4; *see also specific types*
benefit (and good) 2, 4, 19–20, 32–57; defining 4, 19, 32–5; NSA surveillance programs and 28; policy making based on 55–7;

pragmatism and 35–8; principals and 38–44; promoting the common good 120–1
border and cross-border effect 40–1
BP: Deepwater Horizon and 70–1; *Exxon Valdez* disaster and 71
Breyer, Justice Stephen 61
Browns Ferry nuclear plant 70
Buffett, Warren 91
Bush (President George W.) and his administration 19, 50, 64, 82, 85, 93, 106

Califano, Joseph 109
California, Tuolumne River dam 43, 74
Caligula (Roman Emperor) 23
cancer: asbestos and 60; European Union and chemicals causing 73; Tacoma copper smelter and 67; Three Mile Island incident and 35
cannabis/marijuana 20, 33, 113, 114, 116
care (ethics of) 16
Carter, President Jimmy, and administration 108–9
categorical imperative (of Kant) 13
chance, equal 81
chaos theory 37, 38
chemicals affecting health, EU and 73
Cheney, Vice-President Richard 64
choices, making *see* decisions
civil disobedience 102
Climate Research Institute, University of East Anglia 135
Clinton (President) and administration 13, 25–6, 65, 97–8
commitments, honoring 97–111

common good, promoting the 120–1
commons, tragedy of the 48
community: failure 92–3; government
        role in community life 86;
        interdependent 90, 91; living in
        139–43
compassion 137–9
conflicting norms 129–30
Congress 3, 29, 30, 31, 109, 122;
        federal government funding and
        143; Guantanamo Bay prison and
        50; immigration bill 33
Connecticut, New London
        Development Corporation 63
consent: informed 13; paternalism
        based on 115–16
consequences (and consequentialism)
        10–12, 14, 35, 36, 106, 127; event
        tree analysis and 70; *see also*
        non-consequantialism
Constitution and constitutions 32, 86,
        100, 109, 120, 142; prohibition
        and 112
contingency evaluation 46–7
copper smelting and arsenic 66–7
cost, opportunity 74
cost–benefit analysis 20, 21, 23, 43, 45,
        49, 58, 61, 74, 75
cost–effectiveness analysis 20, 61–2, 89
countries and the cross-border effect
        40–1
criminal/unlawful and offensive
        behavior 38, 116, 125
cross-border effect 40–1

dam, Tuolumne River 43, 74
data collection: raw 131
decisions/choices (and making them) 7;
        benefits 19–20; moral 2, 12–13,
        15, 17, 18, 120, 129; rational vs
        irrational 48, 76; status quo 1, 76,
        77, 137
Declaration of Independence 86, 107,
        108, 120
Deepwater Horizon 70–1
deficit (budget) 41; reduction 25–6, 36,
        138
deliberative democracy 140–1
democracy 107, 121, 124; deliberative
        140–1; Iraq 19, 20; liberal 140;
        representative 67–8, 122
Democrats 113
Denver Income Maintenance
        Experiment 32–3

deontology 10, 12–13, 13–14, 14, 15,
        16, 18; mixed deontological
        theory 14
deviance from law 101–2
Devlin, Lord Patrick 117, 118, 119
discernment, moral 134–5
disciplining emotions 24–5
discount rates 73–4
discrimination and anti-discrimination
        law 84–5, 93
discussions and discourse 2–3, 4–5,
        7–31
distribution (of resources), fairness in
        82–3, 87, 88, 91, 92, 93–5
divine law 100, 108, 117; Islamic/
        Sharia 13, 103, 108

East Anglia (University of) Climate
        Research Institute 135
economics, behavioral 75–8
effect: difference between benefit and
        32; standards based on 125–6
effectiveness 2, 4, 20–1, 58–75;
        defining and measurement 4, 20,
        58; limitations on reach of 68–72;
        NSA surveillance programs and
        28–9; popular control and 63–8
effort, to each according to 80
emotions 24–8
enforcement of morality 117–18,
        126–7
entitlement 18, 77–8
environmental regulation/policy (and
        the Environmental Protection
        Agency) 34, 46, 62, 66, 67, 99
equality 83–4, 86, 91, 95, 135; standard
        of equal shares for all 80, 83
European Union and chemicals
        affecting health 73
event tree analysis 70–1
existence value 42–4
experts (judgments and preferences of)
        51–3; lay persons and 53–4, 65–6
external assumptions 105–9
Exxon Valdez disaster 46, 71

facts, agreement or disagreement about
        130–2
fairness 2, 4, 21–2, 79–96; assessments
        93–5; definition/meaning 4, 21,
        79–80; in different contexts 92–5;
        NSA surveillance programs and
        29–30; standards 80–1, 83–6
Fanny Mae 104

fault tree analysis 70
federal government funding (from 2013) 143
Feinberg, Joel 116
fidelity 2, 4, 22–3, 97–111; definition/measures 4, 22; NSA surveillance programs and 30; reciprocal/mutual 102–3
fiduciary relationship 110
Fifth Circuit Courts of Appeals 62
fiscal year: 2012, and the fiscal cliff 122; 2013 143
food stamps 22, 45, 80, 93, 120
foreign countries and the cross-border effect 40–1
foretelling the future 36–7
Frankena, William 14
Freddie Mac 104
free market 45, 76, 123; the state and 124
freedom 86; *see also* liberty
Fried, Charles 121
Fuller's *Morality of Law* 100–3
future: foretelling/prediction 36–7; generations, concern for well-being 41–2; uncertainty 56

gains vs losses, value placed on 75–6
Gates, Bill 59, 91
Gates, Robert (Secretary of Defense) 104
gays and lesbians 16, 119
Geertz, Clifford 35
Genetic Information Nondiscrimination Act 85
George, Robert 119
Georgia–Tennessee and the cross-border effect 41
Gilligan, Carol 16
Global (Great) Recession 36, 89, 93, 136
God: honoring commitments and 107, 108; justice and 79; Ten Commandments and 13
good *see* benefit
goods *see* property; resources and goods
Gore, Al 82
governance 101, 112, 121, 122, 126, 129, 130; legitimacy 55, 117; Nazi Germany 102; respect for persons 97
government and state: community life and role of 86; free market and the 124; harm to others and its

prevention by 125, 126, 127; responsiblities acquired by own actions 99; structural requirements and obligation 100–3; watchdog state 86, 117; what we want them to do 2
grandfathering 99
Grassley, Senator Charles 97, 98, 99, 104
Great Ape Protection Act 40
Great Recession 36, 89, 93, 136
Guantanamo Bay prison 49–50
Gutmann, Amy 113, 140, 141

Happyville 51
harm 125–6; continuum between benefit and 35; defining 115; harm to 114–15; to others 114–15, 125, 126, 127; to self 115–16; to society 118–19; thin vs thick conception 35
Hart, H.L.A. 119
health, EU and chemicals affecting 73
health care 52, 65, 79, 82, 89, 94, 110, 127, 142; *see also* Medicare
health insurance 8, 79, 84–5
HIV and AIDS 52, 62
Hobbes, Thomas 87
homosexuals (gays and lesbians) 16, 119
honoring commitments 97–111
horizontal norms 132
Huckabee, Governor Mike 142
human life 88; statistical, value for 45–6
humility, embracing 135–7
Hussein, Saddam 19, 130

ideology 136, 137
imperfect information 72–5
implied obligations 103–5
income (wages and salaries): cuts to minimum 99; differentials/variations between individuals 45, 80, 81; guaranteed 32–3
individual (personal) attributes 85–6
individual (personal) autonomy 44, 87, 88, 89, 90, 91, 92, 95, 121
individual (personal) behavior *see* behavior
individual (personal) judgments 12, 17, 44, 128
individual (personal) preferences 9, 41, 42, 44–50, 51, 52, 53, 54, 123, 124

individual (personal) respect *see* respect
informed consent 13
instrumental vs intrinsic value 33–5,
74
insurance: genetic information and 85;
health 8, 79, 84–5
intelligence-gathering 28, 29
interdependent community 90, 91
interest: public 44, 139, 140; self-
interest 45, 107, 121, 136; special
(groups) 65, 139
internal morality of law 100–3
intrinsic vs instrumental value 33–5,
74
Iran 103, 108; Iran-Contra affair 101–2
Iraq 19–20, 24, 38, 62, 104, 130
irrational vs rational choices 48, 76
Islamic (Sharia) law 13, 103, 108

Jesus of Nazareth 107–8, 108
Jonsen, Albert 15
judgments, moral/ethical 8–10, 16, 17;
discernment with 134, 135, 136,
139, 140, 142; expert *see* experts;
individual 12, 17, 44, 128;
legitimacy and 112–14, 115, 117,
118, 119, 120, 127, 128; welfare-
based utilitarianism and 11
justice 86, 95; as fairness 90–1; multiple
criteria 80–3

Kaldor–Hicks criterion/standard 59
Kant, Immanuel 13, 14, 75, 98
King Jr, Martin Luther 108

law (and legal systems) 100–3;
constitutions and 100; divine *see*
divine law; fairness and 92–3;
higher 100, 109; Islamic/Sharia
13, 103, 108; judgments in, ethical
judgments vs 112–13; morality
and 100–3, 107–8, 126–7; natural
100, 109, 117, 118; *see also*
legitimacy
lay persons (and their preferences) 53;
experts and 53–4, 65–6
legal issues *see* law
legitimacy 2, 4, 23, 112–29; definition
4, 23; governance 55, 117; NSA
surveillance programs and 30;
sorting through policy options
124–8; *see also* law
lesbians and gays 16, 119
liberal democracy 140

libertarianism 44, 87, 88, 127
liberty baseline 86–8, 88, 89; choice
between welfare baseline and
90–2
life *see* human life
liver transplantation and alcoholism
84
Locke, John 87
losses vs gains, value placed on 75–6

McCarthy, Cormac 79
Madison, James 87, 142
majoritarianism 122, 123, 125, 126
marijuana/cannabis 20, 33, 113, 114,
116
market transactions and preferences
expressed through markets 44–50;
see also free market
marketplace: perfecting the 123–4
Meacham's *American Gospel: God, the
Founding Fathers and the Making of
a Nation* 131
means, effective 61–3
means-and-ends reasoning 11
Medicaid 22, 80, 89, 120
Medicare 26, 54, 85, 89, 93
merit, to each based on 80
Metropolitan Transit Authority budget
in Nashville 138
military issues: gays and lesbians 119;
harm to other side 40; honoring
commitments 97–8, 101–2, 104
Mill, John Stuart 11, 114, 115
morality: in decision-making 2, 12–13,
15, 17, 18, 120, 129; law and
100–3, 117–18, 126–7; moral
discernment 134–5
mortgage crisis, subprime 84, 104
mutuality 141; in fidelity 102–3

Nardella, Jena 144
Nashville Metropolitan Transit
Authority budget 138
National Guard 22
national security 65, 83, 102; National
Security Agency (NSA) 28–30
natural law 100, 109, 117, 118
Nazi Germany 74, 102; Nuremberg
trials 30, 107
need, to each according to 80
negative effects-based standards 125
New London private property
purchases 63, 105
Niebuhr, H. Richard 15

nightwatchman (watchdog) state 86, 117
NIMBY (Not-In-My-Backyard) problem 60, 76
9/11 attack 19, 26, 28
non-consequentialism 12, 14, 77, 78
norm(s): benchmarks and 129–30, 132; conflicting 129–30; external/ international 105–9; horizontal 132; vertical 132
normative ethics 7
Not-In-My-Backyard (NIMBY) problem 60, 76
Nozick, Robert 86, 87
nuclear power plants 37, 60, 68–70; Three Mile Island 35, 69, 70; *see also* radioactive waste storage and disposal
Nuremberg trials 30, 107

Obama, President Barack 30, 50, 79, 90, 131
Obamacare 85
obligations, honoring 97–111
O'Connor, Justice Sandra Day 105
offense to others 116–17, 125
oil spills: Deepwater Horizon rig 70–1; *Exxon Valdez* 46, 71
opportunity costs 74
others: harm to 114–15, 125, 126, 127; offense to 116–17, 125; response to 14–17, 18–19
outcomes, tradeoffs among 58–61
ownership of problems 112–29

pain in animal experimentation 39
Pareto principle/efficiency 47, 59, 60
passion 137–9
paternalism 115–16
Patriot Act 30
pay: to each according to ability to 80; willingness to *see* willingness to pay; willingness to accept payments 76, 77
Pelosi, Nancy 84
perfection: marketplace 123–5; unattainable standard of 72
personal... *see* individual
popular control and effectiveness 63–8
Portney, Paul 51
positive effects-based standards 125
pragmatism 3–4, 35–8, 106; benefit and 35–8; principle vs 43
predicting the future 36–7

preference(s): individual 9, 41, 42, 44–50, 49, 51, 52, 53, 54, 123, 124
preference-based utilitarianism 11–12, 41, 44–50
presumed obligations 103–5
Prince William Sound, *Exxon Valdez* disaster 46
principle(s): benefits and 38–44; pragmatism vs 43
prison: Guantanamo Bay 49–50; treatment of prisoners 106–7
private property *see* property
private schools 81, 82
probability and uncertainty: difference between 72
problems/problematic situations 8; ownership 112–29
prohibition (alcohol) 112
property, private 104–5; New London purchases 63, 105
public interest 44, 139, 140
public schools 45, 81, 93, 120
public service, ideal of 109–10
public will, enacting 121–3
purpose and fairness 95

radioactive waste storage and disposal 22, 54, 61, 69–70; *see also* nuclear power plants
Rasmussen Commission 69, 71
rational vs irrational choices 48, 76
raw data collection 131
Rawls, John 16, 90–1, 132, 140, 141
reasoning 7, 91; emotion and 24, 27; means-and-ends 11
reciprocity 140–1; in fidelity 102–3
reflection 2, 3, 7–8, 10, 17, 18
reflective equilibrium 16–17, 132
religion 13, 131, 141, 142; honoring of commitments and 103, 107–9; law and *see* divine law; *see also* God
representative democracy 67–8, 122
Republican Party 30, 50, 113; autonomous individual story at Tampa 2012 Convention 90
resources and goods: fairness in distribution of 82–3, 87, 88, 91, 92, 93–5; stewardship of 58–75; *see also* property
respect (for humans/persons) 97, 98
response (to others) 14–17, 18–19
responsibility 16, 103, 108, 126; to God 108; the responsible self 15

results (of our acts), achieving 10–12
right and entitlement 18, 77–8
risk assessment 10, 51, 68–72, 73–4
Roosevelt, President Franklin 101
Ross, W.D. 129
Ruckelshaus, William (EPA
    administrator) 67
rules: obeying 12–14; rule utilitarians
    12
Rumsfeld, Donald 136

Sagoff, Mark 49
salary *see* income
Sandel, Michael 51, 81
schools 21, 45, 81, 93, 120; magnet 81,
    138
secrecy 29, 65, 131
self: harm to 115–16; responsible 15
self-interest 45, 107, 121, 136
Sellers' *Public Ethics: American Morals
    and Manners* 132
sexual orientation, gay and lesbian 16,
    119
Sharia law 13, 103, 108
Snowden, Edward 28, 30
Social Security system 21, 26, 54, 77,
    85, 93, 120
society: to each in recognition of
    contribution to 80; fairness based
    on benefit to 82; harm to 118–19
soldiers *see* military issues
special interest groups 65, 139
state *see* government and state
status quo, choosing 1, 76, 77, 137
stewardship of resources 58–75
structural requirements and obligation
    in government 100–3
subprime mortgage crisis 84, 104
Sunstein, Cass 53
Supplemental Security Income program
    21–2
survey techniques in contingency
    evaluation 46–7, 73–4
surveyor's benchmarks 5, 132–3

Tacoma, arsenic and copper smelting
    66–7
talking about ethics 8–10
teleology 10–11, 15, 16, 19
Ten Commandments 13
Tennessee: Georgia and, and the cross-
    border effect 41; Metropolitan
    Transit Authority budget in
    Nashville 138

terrorism 19, 28, 68; 9/11 attack 19,
    26, 28
Thompson, Dennis 113, 140, 141
Three Mile Island 35, 69, 70
torture 106, 107
Toulmin, Stephen 15
tradeoffs among outcomes 58–61
tragedy of the commons 48
Tuolumne River dam 43, 74

uncertainty: difference between
    probability and 72; in future
    predictions 56
University of East Anglia Climate
    Research Institute 135
utilitarianism 11–12, 44–53, 114; act
    12; preference-based 11–12, 41,
    44–50; rule 12; welfare-based 11,
    50–3

value(s) 2–3; conflict of values 5–6,
    134; contingency value,
    assessment 46–7, 73–4; existence
    value 42–4; information use
    affected by 73; intrinsic vs
    instrumental value 33–5, 74; losses
    vs gains 75–6; for statistical human
    life 45–6
vertical norms 132
Vietnam missing soldiers from the war
    97–8, 99, 104
virtue, enhancing 119–20
Viscusi, Kip 46

wage *see* income
Washington, Tacoma arsenic and
    copper smelting 66–7
watchdog state 86, 117
Weiss, Carol 135, 136, 136–7
welfare (and its provision) 34
welfare-based paternalism 115, 116
welfare-based utilitarianism 11,
    50–3
welfare baseline 88–90; choice between
    liberty baseline 90–2
welfare state 86, 120
well-being: animal 39–40; of future
    generations, concern for 41–2
will (public), enacting 121–3
willingness to accept payments 76,
    77
willingness to pay 44–50, 76, 77, 84,
    123; limits 47–50
workfare 34, 80